PRAISE FOR
THE SCIENCE OF DREAM TEAMS
AND MIKE ZANI

This essential read will help any leader bring out the best in their people and outperform the competition.

—MICHAEL C. BUSH, CEO of Great Place to Work

An indispensable road map to creating high-performing teams who can build a great company, this book is a must-read for anyone who aspires to organizational excellence.

—JIM KOCH, Cofounder and Chairman
of Boston Beer Company

For business leaders concerned about linking their business strategy to their talent strategy, *The Science of Dream Teams* speaks to a relevant problem—our inability to consistently and predictably get the most out of our people—and offers a practical solution.

—LYNDA M. APPLEGATE, Baker Foundation
Professor at Harvard Business School

Mike Zani has much to teach us about team building. In *The Science of Dream Teams*, he generously shares wisdom gleaned from his 20 years of experience helping hundreds of companies optimize their teams.

—ERIC ROZA, CEO of CrossFit, Inc.

One of the most transformative books on building teams I've read in years—each chapter is full of real advice for elevating the performance of your most important asset, your people.

—DAVID CANCEL, CEO of Drift.com, Inc.

The Science of Dream Teams is like Moneyball for managing talent. Read it, and you realize that most of us have been coasting on our most important asset, our people, and relying on our guts. Mike Zani finally shows us how to put science into the talent equation.

—ROBERT GLAZER, *Wall Street Journal* and *USA Today* bestselling author of *Elevate, Friday Forward,* and *How to Thrive in the Virtual Workplace*

A brilliant argument for complementing personal judgment with objective data, this book will forever change the way you build, structure, and motivate teams.

—DAN KENARY, Cofounder and CEO of Mass. Bay Brewing Company, Inc.

As an entrepreneur, I've built countless teams, and wish I had this book and access to The Predictive Index sooner. Mike provides excellent insights that make you look inward to explore your own strengths and weaknesses as a leader—and to properly examine your employees' profiles and data to set your business up for success.

—JOE DE SENA, Founder and CEO of Spartan

Zani is an expert in building exceptional teams. *The Science of Dream Teams* gives an inside look at the tools that great organizations use to bring the right people together so they can do their absolute best.

—CHRIS SAVAGE, Founder and CEO of Wistia, Inc.

The Science of Dream Teams goes beyond just teams. It presented many opportunities for my own introspection and actionable ways for me to improve as a self-aware leader.

—KATIE NG-MAK, VP of the Solutions Partner Program at Hubspot

Aspirational yet practical, *The Science of Dream Teams* is a master class on crafting high-performing teams.

—MOLLY SIMMONS, Founding Partner at McFarland Partners

In the modern war for talent, understanding fit is a critical part of attracting and retaining the right people. A strong assessment capability is an indispensable tool for any leader to use in building great teams, and Mike Zani provides the road map to follow.

—KENT PLUNKETT, Founder and CEO of Salary.com

Zani provides an outstanding road map for navigating the people side of business and brings rigor to talent optimization. Filled with relevant real-world examples, this book hits home with all the challenges today's CEO faces. Zani doesn't leave you hanging; he gives clear next steps to make sure you reap incredible value from every chapter. If you spend your time exploring one book this year, this is the one that will make a difference.

—NANCY MARTINI, CEO of Martini Advisory
and former CEO of The Predictive Index

The Science of Dream Teams is the definitive blueprint on how to hire, develop, and retain top talent.

—MIKE HOGAN, CEO of Paradigm Energy Services

Casting is often said to be the secret of any successful production. Cast well; the director relaxes. Cast badly; the director works way too hard. Mike's book is a dynamic guide not only to successfully staffing any organization but also to keeping the troops engaged and productive. It is also the single best book I have read on self-awareness in a very long time. In clear, accessible language, Mike provides a series of structures that enables anyone to lead and communicate with greater creativity and authenticity. You will feel like you are in the hands of a master who is empowering you to maximum success. This is one to keep at your side for daily reference!

—MICHAEL ALLOSSO, motivational speaker
and communications expert

In *The Science of Dream Teams*, Mike Zani provides a valuable framework that offers best practices to improve any team's chance of success. Recognizing the triggers that lead to one's Back of T-Shirt behaviors is a great reminder for any leader who is committed to continuous improvement.

—SAM REESE, CEO of Vistage Worldwide

Looking for guidance on how to take team building to the next level? *The Science of Dream Teams* deserves a spot on your bookshelf.

—HOWARD COX, Special Limited Partner at Greylock

There's an art and a science to building great teams. Most leaders understand the art to a degree. The science can be more elusive. Mike Zani's *The Science of Dream Teams* breaks down the mystery behind team-building science, or talent optimization. An incredible playbook filled with stories, practical examples, and advice on how to use talent optimization to transform your teams and, ultimately, your company. This is a must-read for all people leaders.

—TRACIE SPONENBERG, SHRM-SCP, SPHR,
Chief People Officer of The Granite Group

A splendid people-management tool for normal times, this book is particularly relevant today. In flowing, easy-to-read language, it explains how managers can better understand people currently on their team, as well as potential hires, in order to put them in the best circumstance to succeed for themselves and the company. *The Science of Dream Teams* is a handbook on people management in the post-pandemic, or any, age.

—KEVIN MCCORMACK, Director of
Communications for North America at WPP

When managing my own organization, I often half-joked, "This job would be a lot easier if it weren't for the people." Moving an organization forward in a positive way can only happen if your team is full of satisfied, motivated, and committed individuals with complimentary skills, working together in support of your mission and your culture. Zani offers a clear and engrossing blueprint to do just that, which includes first doing an uncomfortable, yet critical, assessment of yourself.

—BOB BOHNE, former President of Cold Chain Technologies

Zani's refreshing candor and clear writing make this book an easy and compelling read, loaded with insights into how to get the most out of your workforce and the conviction to make tough decisions when different talents are needed.

—SCOTT REQUADT, CEO of Talaris Therapeutics

How often one hears "people are our most important asset" and how rarely hiring reflects this. In an engaging and fun book, Zani shows us how to put aside gut feelings and systematically hire and build better teams.

—JUAN ENRIQUEZ, Managing Director
at Excel Venture Management

The Science of Dream Teams demonstrates how businesses can best use data to manage their greatest investment, their people. This is a terrific and easy read, filled with actionable insights and winning strategies for leaders at all levels of a business, not just the executives.

—RICHARD LEVIN, Leader of the Executive
Coaching Practice at CFAR

For years we've known that getting the right people in the right roles, working as effective teams, is crucial for the success of any organization. This book tells you how to do that by applying data and science—using tools, structure, and process, while humanizing through personal stories. Finally, a way to go beyond gut feel and develop your ideal people strategy.

—BEV HALPERIN, Master Chair at Vistage Worldwide

Like a bestselling thriller, Mike Zani's book is a nonstop page turner that I could not put down. It took humility and courage to reveal his own Back of T-Shirt shortcomings (see Chapter 2). The narrative flows cohesively and compellingly with research data, self-deprecating personal insights, fascinating stories of business successes and failures, and most important, practical exercises for CEOs and senior management teams. Historically, talent optimization was considered more art than science. In today's highly competitive and borderless corporate world, integrating behavioral science and principles of human psychology into building and sustaining a thriving, happy, and engaged dream team is the key to enduring success.

—RENÉE KWOK, President and CEO of
TFC Financial Management, Inc.

I really like this book. As soon as he told the story of the two sides of the T-shirt, I was hooked.

—ART PAPAS, CEO of Bullhorn, Inc.

I highly recommend *The Science of Dream Teams.* For more than 35 years, The Predictive Index has been essential to help drive recruiting, coaching, building teams, and managing talent at our company. This book makes clear just how valuable these tools are and how, in today's global economy and highly competitive world, they make the difference between mediocrity and standout performance for your business.

—MARILYNN DUKER, CEO of Brightview Senior Living

THE SCIENCE OF
DREAM
TEAMS

THE SCIENCE OF
DREAM
TEAMS

How Talent Optimization Can
Drive Engagement,
Productivity, and Happiness

MIKE ZANI
CEO OF THE PREDICTIVE INDEX,
WITH STEPHEN BAKER

New York Chicago San Francisco Athens London Madrid
Mexico City Milan New Delhi Singapore Sydney Toronto

1 2 3 4 5 6 7 8 9   LCR   26 25 24 23 22 21

ISBN   978-1-260-47374-2
MHID   1-260-47374-0

e-ISBN   978-1-260-47375-9
e-MHID   1-260-47375-9

Library of Congress Cataloging-in-Publication Data

Names: Zani, Mike, author. | Baker, Stephen, author.
Title: The science of dream teams : how talent optimization can drive
    engagement, productivity, and happiness / Mike Zani with Stephen Baker.
Description: New York : McGraw Hill, [2021] | Includes bibliographical
    references.
Identifiers: LCCN 2021008624 (print) | LCCN 2021008625 (ebook) |
    ISBN 9781260473742 (hardcover) | ISBN 9781260473759 (ebook)
Subjects: LCSH: Employees—Recruiting. | Teams in the workplace. |
    Personnel management.
Classification: LCC HF5549.5.R44 Z37 2021 (print) | LCC HF5549.5.R44
    (ebook) | DDC 658.4/022—dc23
LC record available at https://lccn.loc.gov/2021008624
LC ebook record available at https://lccn.loc.gov/2021008625

McGraw-Hill Education books are available at special quantity discounts to use as premiums and sales promotions or for use in corporate training programs. To contact a representative, please visit the Contact Us pages at www.mhprofessional.com.

*To Conley, my wife, my partner,
and my friend. Thank you for getting
me started thinking about people
and psychometrics and, more
importantly, for supporting my crazy
entrepreneurship. Without you, I would
never have gotten off the ground. 143.*

CONTENTS

INTRODUCTION

In the 1990s, while I was coaching the US Olympic sailing team, a charismatic coach at the University of Tennessee, Pat Summitt, was turning the Tennessee women's basketball team into a dynasty. When she retired in 2012, suffering from early onset Alzheimer's, she was the winningest basketball coach in American history.

One of Summitt's tools for understanding and managing her players was a personality assessment. This was not cutting-edge science. Tests like the Myers-Briggs Type Indicator (MBTI) and the Predictive Index had been around for decades. The point is that Summitt, a supremely confident coach, still had the humility to search outside of her own head. She, of course, had personal judgment about the players, how they would mesh and under which coaching style each one would be most likely to thrive. However, she would also get an outside read, from a tool, hoping it might provide valuable insights.

It did. Armed with behavioral data, Summitt later said, she could see that the star she was recruiting in New York City, a six-foot-two-inch powerhouse named Chamique Holds-claw, was sky-high on leadership and a big risk-taker. A point guard, Kellie Jolly, by contrast, was highly conscientious, a perfectionist. This informed Summitt's recruiting pitch to the players and, later, how she deployed them. When winning narrowly late in games, she wanted the ball in Jolly's hands. Jolly minimized risk. She wasn't likely to throw it away or dribble it off her foot. But when it came to last-minute shots, the coach wanted Holdsclaw, the risk-taker, to launch them. Each player had special strengths and needs, and the assessment gave Summitt insights into what they were.

In 1997–1998, the team headed by Holdsclaw and Jolly rolled the table, winning every game. They ended the season at 39–0 and won the NCAA championship.

When it came to personality science, Summitt worked with the template that Arthur Daniels had created in the 1950s, the Predictive Index.

FINDING TALENT FOR A TURNAROUND

A decade after Pat Summitt coached her talent-optimized squad to the National Championship, I found myself sitting in an insect-infested office with my business partner, Daniel Muzquiz. We were flipping through a thick pile of résumés, utterly flummoxed about which ones might be promising.

Daniel and I had met just a few years earlier at Harvard Business School, where we hatched the fabulous idea of buying used companies with other people's money. We had managed to round up enough capital from investors to buy our first company, a small industrial shop in Westland, a Detroit suburb popularly known as Wasteland. The company, LEDCO, made docking stations and rugged accessories to fit computers into cop cars. It was a steady market. But we had inherited a lackluster workforce of mostly temp laborers, many of whom were missing the drive, skills, and smarts we were looking for.

To turn this company around, we needed to hire high performers. Yet six months into this venture, we still had little idea how to mine that stack of résumés and find the right people. At Harvard, we had learned a great deal about finance and optimized strategy—but next to nothing about spotting, shaping, and deploying human talent.

How clueless were we? In our early days at LEDCO, we unwittingly hired a crime boss who used the company job as cover. (He turned out to be a star employee. Not surprisingly, he was a gifted leader, who read people intuitively and could build culture. I cried when I learned his dark secret.)

Back when we were wading through résumés, Daniel and I were aware that our methods, centered around unstructured interviews and résumés, were little more than shots in the dark. We knew that managers tend naturally to hire people they're comfortable with, which often turn out to be people like them. The process was inefficient and drenched in personal bias.

Somebody, somewhere, we believed, had to know a smarter method for figuring out people. We hunted for answers, and this led us to Vistage, the largest peer advisory group for CEOs. Vistage holds meetings in cities around the world, where small groups of executives share experiences and learnings. Maybe someone there knew how to hire and inspire the right people.

I walked into my first meeting in Detroit, and the host asked a member named Dan Courser to introduce me. As part of my registration a few days earlier, I had quickly taken a six-minute personality assessment. This generated a behavioral profile. I had barely thought about it and never saw the result. But when Dan interpreted this profile to the group, I was stunned, even embarrassed. It had me cold: my extroverted style and humor, my drive, but also darker stuff—my tendency to bulldoze and sometimes to tune people out. I thought, "Has this guy been talking to my mother?"

Daniel had a similar experience at another Vistage meeting. This was our introduction to personality testing and the Predictive Index—the same personality assessment that Pat Summitt had used to build championship teams.

Tools like this, we saw, could provide insights and direction. Getting a read on each individual, their attitudes about risk and rules and their likely levels of patience and extroversion, fundamentally changed our ideas about managing people. We soon saw that scientific methods could boost us in every area: in recruiting, coaching, building teams, and managing talent. In fact, talent could become our specialty.

This helped us turn LEDCO into a profitable company and a market leader. We sold it. And with that success, we looked to grow. As long as our returns to investors were strong, we could raise more money to buy more companies, and turn them around by using our expanding repertoire of scientific tools to manage the talent.

We bought companies in Florida, Rhode Island, and Texas. But the most enticing company for us was The Predictive Index itself. It was founded in 1955 by Arthur Daniels, who had been introduced to psychometric testing during World War II, specifically to understand why his platoon had managed to fly 30 missions without a single casualty. Daniels made it his career, and the company had honed its behavioral framework for more than a half-century. Its methods had been the subject of hundreds of scientific construct validation studies. The company had a database with millions of profiles and thousands of loyal corporate customers. If we wanted to build a business in the psychology of the workplace, this was a natural target.

We were convinced that the science of human resources was poised to explode. Data detailing humanity's behavior was coursing through networks and into computing clouds, and the trove was growing dramatically. New streams of behavioral data were flowing in from body sensors, social networks, and keystrokes, as well as spoken words harvested by machines. Ever stronger AI could discern patterns in the data and predict human responses. Amazon, Google, and Facebook were deploying these tools to dominate their industries. Moneyball tactics were redefining baseball and turning basketball into an endless barrage of three-point shots. Even sailing was turning into a data sport.

It was only a matter of time before data science rocked human resources. It would arrive, we believed, with an expanding suite of analytical assessments and tools at its core. This information would guide companies in every aspect of dealing with people, from hiring to matching them in ideal teams. Eventually, entire digital platforms would deliver advanced analytics on the human worker. That was the pitch Daniel and I presented to the family and board of The Predictive Index in 2009. They were very nice, but said no. They just were not ready to sell.

Five years later, in 2014, their circumstances had changed. The last living heir of Arthur Daniels, Elizabeth, already in hospice care, suggested selling the company to those two men who were so passionate about her father's system. We bought it within six months. Daniel moved to Massachusetts, and we put the "band" back together.

Our company represents only one niche in an expanding collection of tests and assessments for the workplace. In fact, we use a full panoply of these tools, many of them not made by us. Together, they inform our recruiting, onboarding, team-building, and career planning.

A groundbreaking global movement is applying science to decisions about people. In this new era, sophisticated assessments, data, and software can give managers in any organization insights into humans never before possible. And this practice—what we call *talent optimization*—can make hiring, motivating, and managing people more efficient and effective than ever before. It can help build championship basketball teams, ideal workplace project teams, and well-balanced leadership teams.

The science involves nearly every data company that engages people, in one way or another, while they labor. Facebook, Google, and IBM are all rushing to decipher, predict, and optimize the behavior of humans at work. So are a host of startups, many of which are emerging from research labs at top universities.

In the right hands and in the right culture, this science promises to unlock vast potential in the workplace and beyond. After all, we humans represent our own most valuable resource. The more we learn about ourselves—our drivers, our fears, and our deepest needs—the better we can direct our lives. It's a big deal. And, of course, it's essential for managing our enterprises.

I'm a big believer not just in what our company does but in the broad category of talent optimization. I've done deep dives into the best thinking about the science of people, and closely watched what innovators across this category are building to measure and understand human behavior at work.

From our expanding base outside Boston, we not only use the science to run our own operations, but we also run what amounts to a growing laboratory—one dedicated to decoding the human worker. We're hardly alone, not by a long shot. An entire movement is underfoot in HR. It's a monster market for a digital revolution that's already stormed media, advertising, and commerce.

THE EDUCATION OF A "PEOPLE PERSON"

For me, learning how to manage people is a never-ending story of discovery. Like many others, early in my career, I trusted that I had a competitive edge when it came to figuring people out. I was a people person. Who better to get the most out of every member of a team?

At barely 26 years of age, this was the challenge I faced when I was hired to coach the US Olympic sailing team for the 1996 Atlanta games. The goal was not just to make the team good or great, but the very best in the world. For this, I had to get a bead on each one of these super high performers, many of whom were quirky and all of them intense in their own special way. What did they need to succeed? No less important, I had to figure out how to get them to listen to me. I was not much older than they were and was, in fact, younger than some. In my eyes, I was a wicked good sailor with an eye for sail shape, yet in the Olympians' eyes, I was just a couple of clicks up from lifeguard. How could I get through to them and establish leadership? Like most other leaders, I used my gut and winged it.

Traditional HR professionals, of course, would never admit they wing it. Instead, they insist, as I used to, that certain managers have a "feel" for people and can intuit which ones fit. It is certainly true that some people are good at reading others. It's one of our evolutionary skills. But it doesn't scale to an entire workforce. And it certainly doesn't mean that we cannot benefit from the information and insights now available from a growing science. The future isn't about turning off human intelligence and judgment and bowing entirely to the numbers and charts. The chance we have now is to use both our heads and our new tools.

As players and practitioners at The Predictive Index, we have a special vantage point. In this book, I'll lay out what we've learned about talent optimization and how it lifts morale, builds teams, and turbocharges productivity. I'll show you how science and technology are teeing up a management revolution, and offer ideas and best practices about how to get started in this new and crucially important realm. In each chapter, I will present a detailed explanation of actionable steps, as well as different tools and resources that you can use right away.

The new approach is not simply a matter of tests and data, but also communication and psychology. In a healthy workplace, people have to be able to talk to each other, express themselves honestly, and not guard secrets. They'll only do this in a workplace where they do not get in trouble for telling uncomfortable truths. These are cultural issues, and they're every bit as important as the new sciences. In fact, they work together, because they all contribute to an enterprise that communicates seamlessly, that pulsates with information and insights, one that's aware.

These cultural issues and the seamless flow of information can face big stresses. While we were writing this book, the COVID-19 virus spread around the world and paralyzed large sectors of the economy. The pandemic forced countless companies, including our own, to switch to remote work and slash costs, including payroll. I'll describe the challenges of optimizing talent in a time of crisis and maintaining culture in a remote workforce.

One thing is abundantly clear: It's a lot easier to manage through a crisis with a culture steeped in communication. Quite simply, if people know what's going on, they can respond more quickly. This makes the enterprise more nimble and resilient. And if managers have a read on different employees' personalities and preferences, they can take steps to provide them with what they need, whether it's more space, guidance, and feedback or less of it. Simply put, knowledge about the people in an enterprise, whether from a conversation or an assessment, is invaluable.

Yet this is where I have to raise a cautionary flag. In enterprises marked by distrust, secrets, and ruling cliques, these methods can be poisonous. Take, for example, a school district that's at odds with a teacher's union. Then imagine the teachers' angry response if the district tried to impose cognitive testing on them. If employees do not feel aligned with the company and its goals, if they feel they're being used, they will have fears—legitimate ones—about how this information will be put to use and who has access to it.

Mastery of this science, and doing it right, is quickly becoming a competitive must. If companies create an exciting place to work, where people feel they're in the right roles and positioned to grow, those companies become destinations, attracting greater and better talent. It's a virtuous circle. Recognizing and nurturing great colleagues is at the heart of talent optimization.

The central purpose of this science and this book is to give each person the best possible chance to succeed, grow, and feel fulfilled. That's a stretch goal, of course, but one we consider worthy of pursuit.

THE SCIENCE OF
DREAM
TEAMS

The New HR Tools

At the height of the Industrial Revolution, in 1890, a jeweler in Auburn, New York, named Willard Le Grand Bundy patented the first time clock. This mechanical recorder established time discipline in offices and factories. Workers who punched in even a minute late could be docked pay. The so-called Bundy clocks furnished a vital statistic. With their data, it was possible to calculate the value, whether in tons, bushels, or dollar revenue, of each worker hour. This counting machine helped to launch scientific management.

Over the following century, employers raced to ramp up productivity and to shave off waste. At the zenith of this industrial age, Japanese automakers operated vast plants that ran like clockwork, with just-in-time components reaching the right worker at the right moment. With such optimized processes, manufacturers could calculate the value not just of worker hours but of their minutes.

What stood out about this ever-advancing science, however, was that it focused on the process and not on the individuals engaged in it. The people were nearly interchangeable, like the gaskets and chassis they assembled. In fact, the entire scheme was engineered to make it virtually worker-agnostic. After all, a process whose goal is 99.9999 percent quality must be impervious to the variations in human aptitude and performance. Otherwise, changes in the workforce, for better or worse, would cause quality numbers to fluctuate.

So for a century, the human being was largely left out of scientific management. Humans were too unpredictable and hard to measure. Human resources departments, consequently, developed at the margins of the business. In their offices, usually somewhere down the hall from accounting, they managed risk. They tried to prevent the company from getting sued, and focused on adapting hiring and benefits practices to a slew of regulations and best practices. This was necessary work, but it had nothing to do with strategy. Have you ever seen a triumphant HR executive on the cover of *Forbes* or *Fortune*?

Here's the paradox: While HR developed as a stolid rules-bound bulwark against risk, the asset that HR was managing—human beings—made up by far the most valuable part of all but the most capital-intensive enterprises. Payroll gobbles up about 60 percent of an average company's spending—and people make all the difference. In the Information Economy, a talented and high-functioning team doesn't merely rise to the top. Good teams obliterate the competition.

Yet to this day, most companies' talent strategies still look like boxes in Excel. They're not all that different from the crude numbers generated by Mr. Bundy's clocks.

Why is this? We have not given HR professionals the tools they need to assert their role in strategy. Until recently, they haven't had the mandate or the wherewithal to figure out workers, to spot their strengths, and to deploy them in situations where they're most likely to thrive. We in the information and tools business have failed HR.

Meanwhile, with the advance of technology, loads of other business applications have raced ahead. Logistics is now a precision science, informed by sensors and fine-tuned by analytics. Advertising, long plastered on pages and broadcast to masses, is increasingly calibrated and delivered to the individual. Indeed, we're statistically optimized as consumers, patients, voters, even potential terrorists. But human resources, lacking modern tools and data, has remained largely impervious to science. Until recently, it's been a backwater of by-the-gut thinking, such as:

"Should we hire the guy with the neck tattoo?"
"Mmmm. I can't really handle it."

or:

"Jane kills it in sales. She'll be an OK manager, right?"
"Um. Worth a try, I guess."

These are crucial decisions, and they're often the result of guesswork, bias, and wishful thinking—anything but science.

Now, managers have a broad and fast-growing range of tools and techniques to assess human workers, including themselves. While some of these, such as intelligence tests and personality assessments, have been around for decades, a galaxy of data-generating tools is opening up in the people-managing market.

We'll provide an overview of this expanding tool chest in this chapter. (You'll find more details on the various tools in the Appendix.) But before we start, it's important to note that when it comes to understanding and managing people, including ourselves, the old stuff still counts for more than the new. The foundation of a self-aware enterprise rests upon age-old standards that Plato would recognize: clear and honest communication, fairness, transparency, and accountability. Without a basis in trust, employees will regard the new arsenal of HR tools and techniques as intrusive and controlling, like strings on a marionette. When this happens, workplaces turn toxic, the company's Glassdoor ratings plummet, and star employees skedaddle. That's the opposite of talent optimization.

When managed correctly, though, these tools can help transform an enterprise. The entire field is driven by a bold imperative based upon a new belief: that it's possible at this stage of our economic evolution to manage portfolios of human skills. This is proving, as we'll see, to be transformative. The key is to learn more about each individual.

THE HR MODEL IN SPORTS

If the management model for the industrial age was a hyper-efficient Toyota plant, the template for the Information Age might be a professional sports franchise. In sports, unlike manufacturing, there can be no doubt that the laborers are by far the most valuable resource. There's a simple word for them: talent. And the key to championships is to hire the most talented players and put them where they're most likely to thrive, while organizing them in teams that work together smoothly. Championship squads, from Bayern Munich to the New England Patriots, recruit and deploy their talent more effectively than the also-rans in their leagues.

How do they do it? Through most of sports history, coaches and managers relied heavily on their eyes and gut instincts, supplemented by received wisdom handed down through the generations. Certain managers and scouts boasted of their superior "feel" for talent. Certain players, like Hollywood actors, just looked perfect for the part. What's more, the front offices lacked sophisticated tools and metrics.

In the late 1990s, Billy Beane, a bust as a Major League player, was the general manager of a low-budget baseball franchise, the Oakland A's. As Michael Lewis wrote in *Money-ball*, the bestseller about the data revolution Beane spawned, Beane had no choice but to innovate if he hoped to compete with richer franchises, like the New York Yankees or the Boston Red Sox. Those clubs spent more than four times his budget for talent. Beane would have to figure out how to win with less.

So he launched an HR revolution in baseball. His goal, the same as ours today, was talent optimization. He and his team, which included an MIT stats whiz named Paul DePodesta, studied each player's statistics, including a bunch that few paid much attention to.

Looking back on those early days, Beane remembers hiring a bunch of apparent misfits. One was a burly Canadian outfielder named Matt Stairs. Short and heavy—some might even call him fat—Stairs hardly looked like a prototypical slugger. By 1997, he had bounced back and forth between the minor leagues and the Boston Red Sox, where he had managed to hit only one home run. He was old for a prospect, pushing 28. This made him inexpensive, a big plus for the penny-pitching A's.

Beane and his number-crunching team scrutinized Stairs's minor league stats, including his walks and strikeouts. They ran them through statistical models and concluded that this unlikely Canadian was a potential star. Over the following five years, Stairs smashed 122 home runs for the A's, as he and a host of other apparent misfits and castoffs blended into a division-winning team. "We scored a lot of runs and won a lot of games," Beane says. "And we did it cheaply."

Moneyball turned baseball from a business run on folk wisdom and gut instinct into a science. Since Beane's early triumphs with the A's, the entire baseball industry has raided math and computer science departments at elite universities for premium data analysts. A former industry of he-men has been taken over, to a large extent, by nerds.

To carry out their revolution, they're expanding their tool chest. Every year, they find new things to count, and they continue to install the latest sensors and gauges to measure each player's performance. Since 2015, every Major League stadium has installed a surveillance set-up called Statcast. This enables the new masters of baseball's HR to count the revolutions of each pitcher's curveballs and the degree of dip on his sinker. They can track the exit velocity of a grounder to short or the launch angle of a ringing double off Fenway Park's Green Monster.

They use this knowledge to line up each player for success. The goal is to maximize each person's opportunities, all of which are measured and predicted, of course, statistically.

Now, we're seeing a similar revolution in human resources. This book might as well be called *Moneyball for HR*. What we're witnessing and promoting is the metamorphosis of human management as it pivots from folk wisdom to science.

As science replaces intuition, an entire organization can grow more self-aware. This allows people to be vulnerable, trust each other, and address conflict.

Designing a self-aware organization requires leadership. It is a deliberate act, and must be continuous and unrelenting. That said, there's an expanding universe of choices in this new realm of the knowledge industry.

THE BASIC ARSENAL OF TOOLS

With that, let's turn to the growing arsenal of tools available to evaluate, predict, and deploy human talent. Some are as old as the stats on the back of Babe Ruth's baseball card. Others are just emerging from data labs. We'll start by running through what's available today. In the following chapters, we'll explore how to integrate them for hiring, onboarding, and managing dream teams. For an even more detailed look at each, please see the Appendix.

Cognitive Assessment

Intelligence, as measured by a cognitive assessment, is the single best predictor of job performance. It's not new, by any stretch. Central to success, it's a prime metric (even if you set it to different numbers than IQ, as we do). Cognitive scores are to the workplace what the 40-yard dash is to football.

I hate to say this because, as we all know, such tests are social, ethical, and legal powder kegs. They tend to favor the privileged classes, people raised without anxiety about food and shelter and whose parents used large vocabularies, read to them, and found them tutors.

What's more, a standard 12-minute cognitive test, whether ours or a competing assessment, measures only selected slices of human intelligence—the brain functions that spot patterns and solve complex problems quickly. There are all kinds of other intelligence, as we'll see. In workplaces, the teamwork of dream teams is built upon emotional intelligence, communication skills, and imagination, not to mention humor.

Despite all those caveats, the core cognitive skills are fundamental. The central challenge is to implement and manage these tests with fairness and sensitivity, while respecting privacy.

Each company, then, must figure out for itself how to benchmark for cognitive skills. This will vary from one job to the next. For some positions, say chief scientist, the cognitive score may weigh heavily. For others, like sales, a person's social skills and work habits might count for more. I'll return to the implementation of cognitive assessments in Chapter 8, when we discuss hiring for dream teams.

For now, in assembling the new HR toolbox, just keep in mind that while some of these assessments are optional, the cognitive assessment is a mainstay. The question is not whether, but how to put it to work.

Behavioral Assessment

Like cognitive, behavioral assessments (including our own) have been around for decades. They measure candidates' cultural fit and are essential for molding high-performing teams. Each assessment describes a personality, providing insights into how each team member will interact with others and adjust to change.

You could argue, as many do, that for centuries, great managers have been gathering this intelligence the old-fashioned way—by talking, listening, and observing. This is true. Many of us are gifted at reading signals. A good manager might see that one software developer prefers to work alone, or that a certain designer seems to come alive in small teams. Trouble is, not all managers are equally gifted. And each one, good or bad, is also attached to an ego and a background. These create biases. We all have them. What's more, while a truly talented manager might work wonders with a dozen colleagues, or even 50, those people skills don't scale.

So, like their cognitive cousins, personality assessments are a must for talent optimization. Ours is only one in a large and growing group. (If you would like to take an assessment and receive your own report, visit this link: www.dreamteams.io/BA. Your data will not be used for any marketing promotions.)

Competency Assessment

Are people equipped to handle their jobs? What else could they possibly do? Competency assessments attempt to answer those questions. The traditional ones, which have been around forever, measure technical skills and know-how, such as mastery of a computer language like Python or a phlebotomist's technique in drawing blood. Other competency tests, far more complicated, attempt to measure more ethereal values, such as emotional intelligence and leadership potential.

Competency tests are a fundamental piece of a self-aware enterprise. After all, how can an executive team make the right decisions for the organization if they don't know what everybody can do?

Creating competency assessments is an important exercise because it enables executives to visualize the ideal for every job. This is aspirational, but it establishes the path forward for developing talent. It defines the target. These malleable models, etched in software, can become the connective tissue of the enterprise, central to hiring, organizational design, management, and strategy.

While some assessments look forward, others focus on backfilling. Gap analysis presents the template for the ideal distribution of skills, and then highlights those in short supply. That represents a to-do list, whether for recruiters or trainers.

The field of competency assessments is widening as the industry develops new suites of measurement tools and methods, and crunches new streams of behavioral data.

New Data Tools

Most of the assessments we've discussed to this point, whether cognitive, behavioral, or competency, require workers or job candidates to stop what they're doing and take a test. But it doesn't have to be so. If you think about people at work, whether at the computer or heading out to lunch with colleagues, each one is generating megabytes of data. These troves of data describe the words they use and their patterns of movement, friendships, and social networks.

Little surprise then that we have a host of new HR tools to provide new insights from behavioral data. Some record sales calls and process them through an analytics engine to come up with best practices. Others scrutinize the facial expressions, pauses, and word choices of job candidates to gain insights about them. A few scrape data from social networks to spot workers most likely to leave or to hunt for problem behaviors, such as substance abuse. These tools pose serious privacy issues. And without careful use and clear communication, they could undermine morale. That said, the field is growing.

FUZZY STUFF

For all the power of modern data analysis, certain aspects of human behavior remain stubbornly difficult to measure and model. Consider grit, for example. It's the rage in HR. Everyone wants to hire and retain employees with determination and stick-to-itiveness. Business professor Angela Duckworth not only wrote a bestselling book on the power of grit but has gone on to create an entire information and consulting ecosystem around it.

Grit is no doubt important. It feeds engagement, which works like magic on productivity, creativity, and sales—in short, on success. But when it comes to measuring and predicting, grit can become squirrelly. It's hard to pin down.

The military, of course, views grit as essential. But they don't need to measure it. They have a test. It's called "boot camp." Marine recruits spend 13 grueling weeks cut off from the rest of the world at Parris Island, in South Carolina. They go through intense drills and physical training, and they must complete a 54-hour session of simulated combat known as "the Crucible." Leadership can be reasonably sure that those who make it through have ample quantities of grit.

It's true, there are statistical stand-in assessments for grit, such as "conscientiousness." But conscientiousness denotes control and precision, attention to detail. And plenty of people with grit—in all modesty, I'd include myself here—press forward without sweating the rules or details. Grit also seems to correlate with hope, another difficult trait to quantify.

So grit, while valuable, is elusive. This makes it a lucrative market for development and research. In the meantime, plenty of players will develop and market grit detection. As these tools generate data, they'll no doubt improve. But in the early stages of digital boom markets like this one, some players are sure to sell various degrees of hypothesis as truth.

Know Yourself

I f you're a leader of an enterprise, the first step in talent management is to confront questions about yourself. You no doubt have ideas about how you're faring and about the honesty and openness of your team's communication. But how do others see you? They might nod when you talk and laugh at your jokes, but what are they saying when you're not around? What are you missing?

Figuring this out is vital. As we'll see, tools and assessments can help immensely by shining a light on top management's blind spots and unearthing hidden potential. They can illustrate how our reptilian brain and cognitive biases drive us to make decisions that aren't logical or smart. We'll get to them in a few pages.

But the first step is far more basic. It involves confronting our own delusions about ourselves. The first key to building a self-aware organization is to bring leadership's self-image into alignment with perception. A lot of this has to do with a willingness at the very top of the company to learn and listen—and to adjust.

I experienced a rude but invaluable introduction to this concept early in my entrepreneurial career. It was soon after Daniel and I had bought our first company, LEDCO, that James Allen, the Global Strategy leader at Bain & Co., told me about it. He called it "Front of T-Shirt, Back of T-Shirt."

It's a valuable framework. To begin, picture a T-shirt crafted just for you. It's covered with words. On the front is a list of everything you might tout on LinkedIn, things that your mother might use to brag about you to her friends. It includes your achievements and degrees, all of the commendable steps that have lifted you to the lofty position you now occupy. It also celebrates the qualities you're proud of: your drive and intelligence, that knack you have of getting people to listen, your humor. Wearing this T-shirt, you might start to feel pretty good about yourself (at least if you're not concerned about bragging). Pretty much every job you have ever landed was the result of these attributes.

However, there are two sides to the T-shirt. The back is also covered with words, and they're very different. They enumerate what people say about you when you're not around. It's all the stuff they don't dare say to your face. Maybe your jokes are sexist or you play favorites. Perhaps you're in love with your own ideas. Maybe you have bad breath.

The important thing is this: If you can't read the back of your T-shirt, there's a gap, even a chasm, between your self-image and how others see you. This represents a dangerous disconnect at the top of the company. What's more, the stuff on the back of our T-shirts is what stalls our careers, preventing us from reaching our goals, from achieving, in the vision of the gifted consultant Michael Allosso, "You on your best day."

The consequences can be disastrous for companies, and also undermine our personal ambitions. If you're at a consulting firm like Bain, my friend explained, or a top law firm, it's the front of the T-shirt that gets you in the door as an associate.

However, after five or six years, it's time to decide whether to make you a partner. This is a crucial juncture in a person's career.

At this point, the discussion among the partners focuses almost entirely on the back of the T-shirt. If you're full of yourself, in love with your opinions, obnoxious, a bore, or a sexist, there's a good chance you don't think of yourself that way or, at least, you hope that no one notices. But they do. It's the stuff on the back of the T-shirt that keeps people from becoming partners.

With this discussion, it was as if my friend had pried off the spotless counter in my kitchen to expose a space crawling with rodents and roaches. At that point, I was pretty happy with the front of my T-shirt. It was emblazoned with my Ivy League degrees, sailing prowess, and Olympic coaching. I believed I had good communication skills and that people liked me. Those virtues were spelled out, too.

But since the good stuff was only half of the story, I realized that I had to explore the dark side. After all, it's hard to hold people accountable when you, as a leader, aren't accountable yourself. So I embarked on a painful and humbling hunt to discover the words on the back of my T-shirt. In 2007, I hired a CEO coach and asked him to help me in this exploration. He went on a fact-finding mission and performed a 360 analysis. He talked to everyone in my sphere, inside and outside of the company. He also conducted a battery of assessments, including Myers-Briggs, the Birkman, FIRO-B, and the Predictive Index's behavioral assessment.

When he returned with the results, I learned to my dismay that the people I worked with not only spotted a number of my shortcomings. They agreed on them. There was a consensus: I was not always a good listener. This meant that I tended to bull forward with my own ideas, trusting that my charm, humor, and reason would win out. It often did, of course, because I was in charge. But not everyone was happy about it. They had to come up with strategies for dealing with me and getting me to listen. Sometimes it wasn't worth the trouble. When I tuned out, the value of the conversation shriveled to nothing, or even became negative.

The way Harvard Business professor Frances Frei describes it, when people are listening actively to each other and communicating constructively, they're in a "sweet spot." It's often the Back of T-Shirt behavior that gets us off that sweet spot. The trick is to recognize that behavior and stop it before it starts.

For me, this involved understanding my deeply ingrained habits and changing them. When did I tune out? What triggered this behavior? And how could I learn to listen better and be more accountable?

Analyzing my behavior, I identified three different ways I tune out. Trigger #1: In the course of a conversation, an idea can come up and distract me. Without mental discipline, I can slip into "shiny object" mode, during which I go away for a few seconds or even minutes, leaving the conversation on automatic pilot. I may be nodding, but I'm not really there. Trigger #2: I can become too enamored of my own ideas. When this happens, I tune out other people because I am busy refining my own idea or formulating a response. Trigger #3: I have an intolerance of incompetence. If I feel that someone brings nothing of value to a given topic, I just shut off. This is cruel, even nasty, but it happens.

I recently told my friend at Bain about this process and my findings. I was probably a little bit proud. After all, I'd done a lot of digging, and had come up with insights about my weak points. A lot of people don't do this. Yet he insisted that I had let myself off easy, that I should have pushed harder. He pointed to my third trigger. "What's going on there?" he asked. "Do you think they're stupid or incompetent? Why haven't you confronted that? Are you reluctant to have that conversation?"

His larger point is that if you've done your Back of T-Shirt work and feel satisfied that you've got it covered, there's always something else to find, somewhere you can dig deeper. It never ends.

Still, you manage what you know. The key is to recognize the triggers for your Back of T-Shirt behaviors, and respond to them immediately. Here I've made some progress. But the most effective method I've found—the backstop—is to enlist my colleagues. I have given them a safety word and a promise that I will not get mad if they use it. I've asked them to say "Ticonderoga" if they notice me tuning out. It means: "You're doing it again. Stop and listen to me. I'm saying something you've got to hear." When they say that word, I kick myself, but also thank them and snap back into listening mode.

THE PERFORMANCE CHALLENGE

The essence of the Back of T-Shirt exercise is to see yourself through other people's eyes. It involves listening to their feedback and observing interactions closely. But it's also a function of your imagination.

This imagination is especially important for the next exercise, which involves seeing yourself as others see you, and imagining how they interpret your behavior every minute of the workday. Fact is, as Michael Allosso has pointed out to me, the CEO is constantly under the spotlight. Everyone is looking at you, always. It is relentless.

For example, you walk into the office and smile at one colleague, exchange a friendly word, and then walk past another, ignoring her while beelining to your office. What conclusions can be drawn from that? It can fuel discussion in the lunchroom. During a meeting you check your text messages while someone is talking. People notice. Your shoulders sag during a VP's PowerPoint presentation. What does that mean? Do you commute with someone? Who are you having lunch with? What does that say about your relationships with them?

I could go on and on. It's a bit like the Kremlinology that Russia-watchers developed during the Cold War. Who's sitting next to the Secretary General? Is he on the rise? The guy who was there last week is out of the picture. Did he get bumped down? Sent to a gulag? Shot? This was an important channel of intelligence, and it informed Cold War policy.

A similar analysis goes on in every workplace. That is why the CEO and other leaders have to be not just authentic, but also performers. People are watching closely. A leader must project the right messages: focus, listening, caring. Everything must be on. Allosso calls it "Showtime." It can be exhausting. But this positive energy and strong focus set the tone for the entire enterprise.

I should add here that your energy, no matter how positive, can also disturb team chemistry. Your job, of course, is to make your colleagues stronger and smarter. But you might notice, or learn from others, that when you sit down with them at a meeting, they become dumber and weaker. A leader can destroy value simply by walking into a room.

Some employees retreat when the leader enters the room, keeping their opinions to themselves. Others might exchange toxic eye rolls with colleagues. A few might step up their participation, becoming more argumentative.

Part of knowing yourself involves carrying out some research on your effect on others, learning how the dynamics change, what triggers those changes, and how you can adjust. Sometimes it's best just to leave teams alone.

EMOTIONAL INTELLIGENCE

Do you sometimes feel like slamming a door or yelling at a colleague, and not know why? That's an issue of so-called emotional intelligence, or EQ. It has to do with understanding your emotions. If you have gaps in this area—and most of us do—they're likely to show up on your Back of T-Shirt. This is because even if we don't understand our moods and what triggers them, others do. They see and feel the impact. It might be pursed lips or a fit of pique at a meeting, or perhaps a pattern of passive aggression. However and whenever they show up, emotions have a big impact on the business.

Recognizing our emotions is central to knowing ourselves and crucial in business. After all, the greatest tests we face as leaders come in times of crisis—when markets crash, products fail, and accidents happen. These are sure to be moments when emotions are surging. It's important to recognize those emotions and understand the impact they have on how we process information and deal with others, whether colleagues, customers, or the news media. If our emotions remain mysterious to us, we face the moments of greatest stress harboring a dangerous unknown inside our heads.

An EQ assessment, at least in my experience, does not deliver instant and compelling insights. Where other assessments, including Myers-Briggs and Predictive Index, can sometimes lay you bare, the EQ simply raises questions. Not long ago, as research for this book, I took one and later puzzled over the results. One of my lower scores was in enthusiasm. Huh? That didn't sound like me.

The value of the assessment comes not from the results, but from the discussion with the facilitator. These are professionals with a certification for psychological counseling. I worked with Heather Haas, president of ADVISA, a consultancy in Carmel, Indiana. This type of session, it turns out, feels very much like time with a caring shrink. At the end of the day, the focus is on our swirling emotions. Some of them are dark, many of unknown provenance. They involve our fears, insecurities, childhood experiences. Coming to grips with EQ requires a deep dive.

For a taste of what's involved, here's one example of what I came away with about myself. I'd been working for 15 years on Front and Back of T-Shirt issues and really didn't expect much further enlightening. But this was an aha insight, and it came from just a half-hour mini session of training.

The test itself didn't tell me much. It gave me high marks for self-regard and problem solving, but a lower score on empathy. I wasn't sure what it meant.

The scores indicate, Haas said, that I'm comfortable in my own skin and have confidence in my judgments and my ability to deal with issues decisively. These aren't bad qualities for the CEO of a fast-moving company. But the trailing empathy, she pointed out, might lead me to brush past people who are struggling to wrap their arms around change and are unhappy or unsettled about it. In that sense, I may lack empathy.

Why does it matter? The easy part of change, Haas said, is making the decision and getting started. What is often harder is the follow-through, making sure it sticks, and dealing with issues that arise along the way. If I, as a confident and problem-solving CEO, fail to slow down to consider other people's feelings about the change, they may not be entirely onboard in the coming months. "That's when you need people's genuine commitment," Haas said. "You build that on the front end by developing empathy."

There can also be a disconnect when a person who is apparently friendly and open behaves differently when the pressure is on. After all, someone like me in happy times is walking through the hallways, smiling, greeting people by name, intent on giving positive feedback; in short, being a supportive and caring boss. Yet when crisis hits, colleagues may see someone who appears to be focused more on the issue at hand than on them and what they're going through. This could undermine trust.

In future sessions, this would be something to work on. But the important point of focusing on emotional intelligence is not to remake our emotional selves. Instead, it's to tune into what we're feeling, and to recognize the emotions when they manifest, as they inevitably do. The key then is to find constructive ways to express them, instead of letting them express themselves or, for that matter, repressing them.

For example, you've asked a manager to produce a report on a customer before an important meeting. He delivers it only a half-hour before the meeting, and it's clearly been patched together at the last minute. You're angry, and you feel disrespected.

The possible bad responses:

1. You call his line, tell him what a miserable job he did, threaten to fire him, and hang up loudly.
2. You call his boss, scream at her, and tell her you expect better from her team.
3. At the meeting, you flip through the presentation impatiently and communicate its worthlessness by slamming it down on the table and shooting a poisonous glance at the offender.

The EQ response, by contrast, recognizes the anger and finds an honest and constructive way to communicate it. This might mean stopping by the manager's office, telling him that you're angry because it was an important meeting and you received what appeared to be a slapdash report only minutes before. Maybe he has an excuse, an illness or family crisis. Maybe not. Whatever the case, he comes away with a clear understanding of what you expect and, also, what pisses you off and why.

In this case, the anger is not repressed. Nor does it disappear. But, importantly, it does not dominate the encounter. You remain in control and, ideally, build trust. This is the immense payoff from EQ.

MAPPING OUT THE EXECUTIVE TEAM

Once you have a grip on your current blind spots and corrosive habits, and you have taken a look at yourself through the eyes of others, it's time to examine the rest of the executive team. How well do you know each other, what each of you needs, and, equally important, what gets under each person's skin? What are the optimal work conditions for each person in the C-suite? (If you would like to map out your own team, visit this link: www.dreamteams.io/team. Your data will not be used for any marketing purposes.)

For each member of our senior management team, we conduct a 360 review. We all have to spell out the Front and Back of our T-Shirts and share them with the team. This process is separate from the annual performance review. Otherwise, people might be tempted to cover up their issues for fear that transparency would cost them a promotion or a raise.

This process, again, relies heavily on insights and observations from colleagues. Even in the Data Age, this intelligence is not to be discounted. Great managers develop a sense for others on their teams, how they like to take in information, how one might need more guidance and feedback, while another might prefer to figure things out by herself. We're humans, after all, and reading fellow humans is our specialty.

However, not all managers are skilled at this. And the knack of an exceptional people person doesn't scale. A CEO, after all, isn't likely to hire coaches for the entire senior team, so an assessment can provide a fresh perspective. It might confirm much of what you've already concluded, but add new details, along with suggestions on how to manage your relationships.

PERSONAL ASSESSMENT CASE STUDY: BETWEEN TWO FOUNDERS

This is where the personality assessment adds value. It can illuminate issues between two people who thought they knew each other well, including longtime business colleagues, even spouses. My business partner, Daniel, and I have known each other since business school, and we have been working together, on and off, for some 15 years. You'd think we might not need assessments, but you'd be wrong. Assessments bring to the surface aspects of our personalities that we understand as vague notions. They crystallize them. And they raise this important question: Are you managing the relationship in the best possible way, or merely settling into substandard routines that have grown comfortable over time?

Our charts (Figure 2.1) assign people to 17 different groupings, or behavioral tribes. Daniel and I have some overlap. But we're also very different. I'm a Persuader. I want to lead, imposing my ideas. I want to get in people's faces and communicate. I'm impatient and have less interest than I probably should in operational details. I tend to be casual, sometimes taking it too far.

Daniel is a Venturer. He too wants to lead, but much more quietly. He needs time and space for himself to analyze, and he cares deeply about operations.

That much I could have told you when we were back in graduate school. But the profiles highlight some useful "blind spots." In my case, a number of them come from the Back of the T-Shirt. Our relationship guide zeroes in on them and

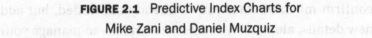

FIGURE 2.1 Predictive Index Charts for
Mike Zani and Daniel Muzquiz

Mike Zani

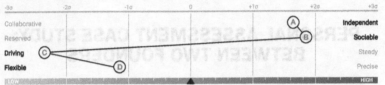

Self Awareness

Your motivating drives tell us that you tend to be:

Extremely	Very	Very	Very
Intense	Outgoing	Independent	Informal
Restless	People oriented	Assertive	Tolerant of uncertainty
Driving	Persuasive	Self-confident	Flexible
May need lots of	**May need lots of**	**May need lots of**	**May need lots of**
Variety	Opportunities to interact	Independence	Freedom from rigid structure
Opportunities to work at a faster than average pace	Social acceptance	Control of own activities	Freedom of expression
Mobility	Opportunities to influence	To be challenged	Opportunities to delegate details

Daniel Muzquiz

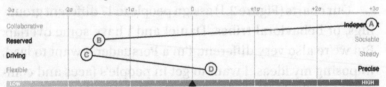

Self Awareness

Your motivating drives tell us that you tend to be:

Extremely	Very	Very	Moderately
Independent	Intense	Introspective	Serious
Assertive	Restless	Matter-of-fact	Diligent
Self-confident	Driving	Analytical	Reserved
May need lots of	**May need lots of**	**May need lots of**	**May need some**
Independence	Variety	Opportunities to reflect	Understanding of rules and regulations
Control of own activities	Opportunities to work at a faster than average pace	Room for introspection	Specific knowledge of the job
To be challenged	Mobility	Freedom from office politics	Freedom from risk of error

provides suggestions on how to manage each other. It warns, for example, that Daniel may be overwhelmed by Mike's eagerness to have a conversation, and that Daniel may back away from our talks, frustrated that I don't get to the point. It adds that I'll likely get frustrated when Daniel delves into what I consider too much detail.

This has helped us figure out how to read and manage each other. It explained why Daniel had the habit of knocking on my door and saying he wanted to discuss something, when it became clear within a minute or two that he had already made the decision and was only going through this "discussion" to sell me on his idea. He'd been through the details (that I ignored) and was eager to avoid the kind of conversation that I liked (and he hated). Understanding this helped me manage these discussions, usually by asking the simplest question: Do you really want to know my opinion, or have you made up your mind?

Many of the observations in our charts are eerily accurate. But even if they weren't, they're useful for kicking off the kinds of conversations top executives badly need—and often avoid. It's extremely helpful to do the following exercise together.

Complete and discuss the following sentences:

It drives me crazy when you _____

_____

I find we work best when we _____

_____

If there's one thing I could change about our working relationship, it would be _____

_____

While it's important to examine the Back of the T-Shirt because it records what we don't see, Richard Levin, a legendary executive coach who recently merged his eponymous firm with the Center for Applied Research, stresses that the Front of T-Shirt remains important. "Even though you want to know what's on the back, you don't want to lose sight of what's on the front," he says. "That's what got you where you are."

After all, your shortcomings don't define you—unless you're blind to them.

THE POWER OF VULNERABILITY

Much of this chapter, as I'm sure you've noticed, deals as much with age-old human interactions as with the new data tools and assessments. This is because honest and open human communication—asking questions and listening—is the foundation upon which everything else I'm writing about in this book is built. If top managers and executives are not ready to explore their own weak points and confront them, you can forget about dream teams. No amount of science can fill that void.

The crucial quality is vulnerability. This is true for every relationship. It's especially challenging, but no less important, for leadership of an enterprise. Many naturally fear that vulnerability will undermine the confidence and authority they need to project. In fact, however, a degree of vulnerability bolsters power because it communicates that everyone, from the bottom to the top of the company, is accountable.

What's more, when leaders act invulnerable and omniscient, others take note and suspect that they're hiding weakness. I saw this while leading sailing teams. Often, I was hired to jump on rich people's race boats to help ensure the win. The captains who screamed the most, almost invariably, didn't know what they were doing. They were the worst sailors and constantly worried that their weaknesses would be exposed. The best sailors, by contrast, kept their calm even in the wildest scenarios.

Being vulnerable can be challenging. Two of Daniel's blind spots, according to his Venturer profile, are tough-mindedness and a tendency to be "overly frank." Knowing and remembering this has been beneficial, especially when I'm on the receiving end of his criticism. It sometimes tests my dedication to vulnerability, but this unvarnished communication is essential.

A couple of years ago at a company holiday party, for example, I said something that was inappropriate. It happens. And it certainly fits in with the blind spots on my profile: the tendency to yammer on and to flout social and professional boundaries.

The next day, Daniel poked his head into my office. "It's my fault," he said. "I've been meaning to tell you. You've always been too casual. You need to hold yourself to a higher standard."

This was true, of course. And with this message, Daniel was updating the Back of my T-Shirt and reading it to me. It wasn't pleasant. It never is. But it's essential. The next steps were not just to own up to my gaffe and apologize, but to make sure I didn't repeat it. That meant analyzing my behavior and the circumstances around it, and figuring out what triggered it. This process never ends.

The more I learn, the more work I see that I need to do. Building a self-aware enterprise, after all, involves far more than uncovering the hard and hidden truths about ourselves at one point in time. That's just the first step. It's just as important to surround ourselves with straight-shooting colleagues—feedback loops—so that the learning never stops.

NEXT STEPS

- Conduct assessments across the workforce, including those for behavior and emotional intelligence.
- Run 360 reviews, starting with the executive team. Incorporate them as a pillar for self-awareness and continual improvement.
- Start discussing the Front and Back of T-Shirt concept with the executive team.
- If you are ready to dive headlong into talent optimization, consider investing in an executive coach. Explore T-Shirt issues together, especially the darker stuff on the back.
- Share at least a couple of the Back of T-Shirt findings with associates, promoting a culture of openness and vulnerability.

Talent Design
Thinking

Through the hot summer of 2018, Elon Musk, the founder and CEO of Tesla Motors, slept for nights on end at his assembly plant in Fremont, California. Musk had vowed that Tesla could gear up production of its Model 3 sedans, rolling 5,000 of them off its assembly line per week. Mastering production of the entry-level Model 3 was crucial to establishing Tesla as a major auto manufacturer. Musk had bet the company on it.

A year earlier, Musk had outlined a vision to turn Tesla from a niche maker of luxury electric cars into a mainstream powerhouse. To build the Model 3, he created a new type of manufacturing line, with robots taking over much of the work. The process was slow getting started, though, and by the summer of 2018, the situation was dire. Tesla had billions in debt coming due. Investors, who had bought in on his vision and driven the company's valuation to the sky, were fleeing. Musk and his team, besieged by glitches and shortfalls, were adapting on the fly, adjusting components, taking robots off certain jobs, and redeploying humans. It was nothing less than an emergency, which was why Elon Musk was sleeping on a cot in his office and wearing the same clothes for days on end.

Think for a moment about Elon Musk. He is one of the great visionaries of our age. As a cofounder of PayPal, he envisioned the future of digital payments. He went on to found SpaceX, a spacecraft manufacturer focused on colonizing other planets. And then, in an effort to save the planet we still inhabit, he founded Tesla and created a booming market for luxury electric vehicles.

Now consider the work Musk was carrying out in that factory. He was dealing with a million details: supply chains, schedules, work flows, the nitty-gritty of engineering. This wasn't vision, but details.

Was Elon Musk born for *that*? Every company has jobs that require different skills and personality types. The challenge is to map out the skills needed and to position people where they can contribute the most. If Tesla planners had worked up a diagram for optimum deployment of human talent, Musk would be firmly in the CEO office, translating his vision into strategy and selling it to employees, investors, and consumers alike. That's his genius. Someone else, an extraordinarily gifted details person, most likely an engineer with Six Sigma Black Belt credentials, would be running the manufacturing operation. The right people in the right places—that is the essence of talent design thinking.

In this chapter, I lay out the staging ground for talent optimization. The purpose here is twofold: first, to figure out the ideal blend of talent for the company's mission; and second, to map the talent currently in place. This requires design thinking.

A good place to start is the Competing Values Framework (CVF). Developed in 1983 by Robert E. Quinn and John Rohrbaugh, it models organizational culture and strategy. It

divides the workforce into behavioral quadrants.* The organizing principle of that scheme has become a standard in the
industry. A number of assessment companies, including The
Predictive Index, divide people into four similar groupings.
Each version has its own nomenclature and its own nuances
of classification and definition. They're like different dia-
lects within a common language. To keep it simple, I'll use
our company's CVF (Figure 3.1). It's the one I know best. But
the process of creating a CVF for a workforce and using it as
a design tool will also function on many of today's platforms.

FIGURE 3.1   The Behavioral Quadrants of the CVF

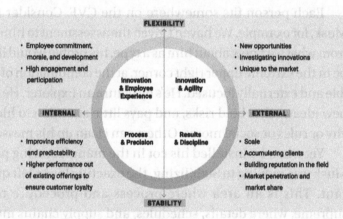

The fundamental metrics of the CVF are based on a person's need for order (stability versus flexibility) and sociability
(internally versus externally focused). People on the left side
of the chart, both above and below, need more order or stability. Many of them pay greater attention to the details. Those on
the right, by contrast, tend to be more flexible, looking more at

---

* In their original study, Quinn and Rohrbaugh labeled them Clan, Adhocracy,
Market, and Hierarchy.

the big picture. Switching the perspective to the Y axis, those on top are more externally focused on people, while those in the lower two quadrants are more internally focused on running successful systems.

We call the resulting quadrants Cultivating (Teamwork & Employee Experience), Exploring (Innovation & Agility), Producing (Results & Discipline), and Stabilizing (Process & Precision). This chart is, in effect, a map of people. It's important to stress that there are no good or bad scores in personality profiles or on the CVF. Some people, you'll see, end up close to the middle, with no clear tag. That's not a problem. They have a dose of everything. They are malleable and serve as valuable connectors.

Each person fits somewhere on the CVF. Consider Elon Musk, for example. We haven't given the assessment to him. But from what we know about him as a type, his profile would likely be in the extreme upper right corner, at the combination of flexible and externally focused. He's by nature an Explorer. He tries new ideas, takes bold risks, and pays little attention to hierarchy or rules or social mores. Others can clean up his messes.

Yet when he installed his cot in the manufacturing plant, Musk was moving to Stabilizing, the exacting lower left quadrant. This is an area where process and procedure reign supreme, where details, schedules, and supply chains matter a lot. Elon Musk was working far outside of his sweet spot.

To his credit, Musk appears to be a talented enough leader to adapt. One of his skills is versatility. By late 2020, the Tesla factories were churning out half a million cars, and the stock shot up by a factor of seven. Musk was on top of the world. Yet for Musk, diving into the process had been torturous. In an interview with *Bloomberg Businessweek*,* he called the expe-

---

* https://www.bloomberg.com/news/features/2018-07-12/how-tesla-s-model
-3-became-elon-musk-s-version-of-hell.

rience the "most excruciatingly hellish several months that I have ever had."

MAPPING INDIVIDUALS

The goal in this chapter is to guide readers in mapping the personalities in an enterprise. With this map in hand, it is easier to see if employees are in the right jobs. Someone with an Explorer profile, for example, is more likely to thrive in a post that requires strategic thinking, and probably is ill-suited to the detail work of accounting. Creating an enterprise-wide CVF is the first step in placing each person in a position where they're most likely to prosper. Later, using the same chart, we'll be able to see if each company has the right behavioral blend for its mission.

The first step is to come up with the data points. Those will be the dots representing each employee, which will spread across the four quadrants of the CVF. You create those dots by giving everyone in the enterprise a psychometric assessment, either from PI or one of our competitors. (For details on the various players, see the Appendix.) Within the PI platform, algorithms automatically deploy assessment results on the CVF, showing the psychometric profile of the entire workforce. The software can also determine the psychometric identity of each team and business unit. But even without these algorithms, it's possible to approximate this analysis manually. The coordinates of each profile suggest that person's place on the map. And by color-coding the points, a practitioner, often a consultant, will be able to signal the nature and proclivities of teams and business units.

Before we start moving the pieces, we have to understand the psychometric groupings—what those dots on the CVF are telling us. Its basic units are the four quadrants.

Explorers: Our name for those in the Innovation & Agility quadrant, are outgoing and risk-taking. Explorers are well-represented as founders of startups. Apple's Steve Jobs, like Musk, would likely be an Explorer. He pushed his own ideas, engaged with the outside world, and didn't pay much attention to rules. At the same time, though, he was a stickler for process, and unlike many in the Explorer quadrant, highly patient. All of us, after all, carry blends of these human drives.

Producers: These people are in the Results & Discipline quadrant. You'll find lots of them in investment banks, hedge funds, and manufacturing. Jack Welch, the numbers-driven CEO of General Electric,was a prime example. Like Explorers, Producers are outgoing, but they tend to be more focused on beating the competition than generating new ideas. They prize statistics, metrics, and, above all, results.

Cultivators: Their quadrant, Teamwork & Employee Experience, is on the upper left side of the chart. They tend to be more inward focused and usually less famous. Cultivators focus on nurturing community. They collaborate. Many have the potential to be leaders but thrive in a supporting role. Oprah Winfrey, while a leader and CEO, has the skills of a Cultivator. She draws value from the people she works with and is exceptional at partnering, whether with authors or companies she believes in, like Weight Watchers.

Stabilizers: They're in the Process & Precision quadrant, in the lower left corner. These are the detail people I referred to earlier. They prefer a steady and reliable environment, with norms and a clear hierarchy. Accountants and software coders are often Stabilizers. Perhaps the model for this group is W. Edwards Deming, the engineer and industrial consultant who helped develop the statistical quality processes adopted by Japanese industry after World War II. He didn't call attention to himself, and he was virtually unknown in the United States for much of his long career. But his focus on statistics and process led to the rise of Japanese automakers, and these methods eventually spread to the rest of the world.

Every company needs the skills from all four quadrants. But all too often, people's personalities don't jive with their jobs. We all know examples, at work and among our friends. The archetype would be someone who dutifully follows the family tradition to become a doctor or lawyer, yet still dreams about writing screenplays.

Consider a member of the marketing team who seems a bit different from his colleagues. Unlike most of them, his dot on the CVF is firmly in the Stabilizer quadrant, in the lower left. These are the process-oriented people who often work in tech. Now there's nothing wrong with having a Stabilizer in marketing. Details matter. But let's assume that this person, while a middling performer, seems to thrive when optimizing marketing content for search engines. Given his CVF and this observation, it might make sense to propose a move into IT— where he could become a star (and also make more money).

People in themselves are usually blends. Visionaries, for example, aren't blind to details. It's just that details aren't their natural focus, so dealing with them feels more like work.

THE PSYCHOMETRICS
OF AN ENTERPRISE

Look at a company through the lens of human resources, as a large and complex deployment of personalities and behaviors (not to mention salaries). Which ones fit the company's mission and are positioned to do their best and most enthusiastic work?

In some cases, the needs are clear. A hospital, for example, needs loads of people in the lower left quadrant. In that line of work, details can spell the difference between life or death. Doctors' ruling credo is the Hippocratic oath, along with the maxim "First, do no harm." Established routines, whether washing hands for 20 seconds or counting out the precise dosage of anesthesia, are crucial. Quality control hinges on everyone following the same rules and checklists.

Most startups are the polar opposite. Leaders are often in the upper right quadrant, willing to take risks and not sweating the small stuff. Much like Elon Musk, Uber's founders were fueled by a grandiose vision. So were Airbnb's. They were all too happy to disrupt the status quo and dismissive (to a dangerous degree, in some cases) of rules.

Every company, of course, needs to fashion a blend from all four quadrants. They're all necessary, but to varying degrees. In certain industries, the blends are predictable. In schools, for example, the administrators tend to inhabit the lower-right Producer quadrant. They measure themselves against others. They focus on growth, reaching targets, and selling those successes to the public and the school board.

Teachers are of an entirely different ilk. Most of them are Cultivators. They concentrate on their students' minds, feeling out and forging the best relationships to break through and make an impact. It's only natural that administrators and teachers often find themselves at odds with each other. Their strengths, focus, and priorities all diverge. At times it can feel as if they're from different planets. Yet both skills are essential. So a school district requires a dual-focus strategy, with principals and superintendents who appreciate the strengths of both cohorts.

The trouble for many companies, we find, is that their talent is not aligned to their mission. Some are entirely out of whack. We had a bank client recently who was facing relentless competitive pressure. All kinds of nonbanks, like Voom and PayPal, were offering financial services. Customers under 40 barely ever visited the branches, and couldn't be drawn in with free candy or coffee. Far more than rebranding, the bank needed a bold shift in strategy, with a strong focus on the customers' needs and habits.

When the CEO looked at his bank's CVF, he almost gasped. He had already determined that the challenges called for a strong deployment of talent on the right side of the chart, the Explorers and Producers who face outward. Yet the bank's personnel tilted strongly to the bottom left. Most were people who focused meticulously on process. No matter how hard he pushed toward the new direction, if his team was not designed for that goal, the entire enterprise was going to feel pain. Sometimes there's no way around it.

The dilemma our bank customer faced, however, wasn't simply a matter of balancing its strengths. The bank needed to become good at something it wasn't built for: innovating and taking risks.

It's not easy. Either the CEO would try to fix the team, which required patience and retraining, or he would move into replacement mode, which brings its own share of drama and anguish. We'll discuss how he tackled this challenge in the coming chapters. The point here is to map out the plan. For this, talent design thinking is crucial. It lays out the path for matching talent to strategy.

ALIGNING TALENT

The first step to bringing a company into alignment is to calculate where it should be. What are the key challenges? To confront them, should the company be oriented toward expansion, exploration, new ideas? Or is control and precision more important? Will it require a cohesive and resilient team? What kind of people provide that?

If you pose those questions to executive teams, you often come to a startling conclusion: Some of them don't even agree among themselves about what they're supposed to be doing! Those teams are misaligned.

Misalignment often occurs while adapting to changing markets. Some of the team remains focused on the legacy business, while others look ahead.

Take a Big Three auto executive. She runs a vast organization that has been following the rules and procedures that developed, through accretion, over the course of a century. Yet disruptions loom. The pandemic changed people's commutes, energy markets are in tumult, electric vehicles are on the rise, and increasingly, cars and trucks will be driving themselves. The century-old company will have to chart a new course and execute on it. What blend of skills will fit this mission?

The traditional skills of the car company, typically, are tilted toward the lower right quadrant: Producers. For decades, the entire operation has been optimized for power and efficiency, adding torque, shaving costs, all to compete with a host of global competitors who for decades have been playing exactly the same game. (These people have been warring forever with the engineers, who aspire to produce the car of their dreams.)

Now the CEO is facing new competitors, like Tesla. These companies are run by Explorers. They take ridiculous risks and make extravagant promises. The markets reward them, piling billions into their stock. And this changes the math. With those sky-high valuations, this new breed can sell cars at a loss—and buy market share. How can a traditional automaker compete?

These questions lead to difficult, and often fruitless, discussions. If extinction fears are keeping them up at night, chief executives, as a rule, prefer to keep their own counsel. Mention gaping, existential weaknesses, and their investors get jumpy. So do employees. This is an example where the need for openness and vulnerability collides with powerful market forces, not to mention the executive's survival instinct.

We address this with a 20-question strategy assessment. It allows executives to rate different concerns, challenges, and opportunities, while bypassing the unwelcome conversation. These questions line up with the talent needed to carry them out. For example, if one of the challenges they prioritize is to implement new systems or processes, then they require workers in the Stabilizing quadrant. If, however, they underscore the need to come up with innovations and commercialize them, then they need Explorers. Developing new pricing or distribution options lines up with Producers, while promoting from within to foster a culture of engagement and professional development would naturally be the domain of Cultivators.

In this way, the survey quietly identifies the type of talent they'll need going forward. When they're finished, usually after about 10 minutes, they see a chart that lines up their needs (strategy) in terms of the four quadrants, with the psychometric deployment of their team and its behavioral fit to execute on the strategy.

Today's constant change, much of it driven by technology, makes it more challenging for companies to keep their talent up to date. Everyone must adapt, but this involves bringing the workforce into alignment.

Some enterprises have faced this dramatic change and successfully added and reoriented the talent on their CVF. The Bill and Melinda Gates Foundation pulled it off, starting in 2006. The foundation, barely seven years old at the time, had its mission based on a motto from Bill Gates's father, William Gates Sr.: Humble and mindful. Many of the foundation's early hires were high achievers from top universities, who were willing to fold their ambitions into the greater cause of global health. Many of them would fall in the upper left quadrant: they were Cultivators.

Bill Gates's longtime friend, the investor Warren Buffett had just earmarked a huge chunk of his fortune, some $31 billion, to the foundation, virtually doubling its endowment. To retain its status as a nonprofit and not sit on its billions of dollars, the foundation had to dramatically increase spending. This resulted in a frenzy of hiring, which brought in dozens of leading experts and entrepreneurs from around the world.*

This new wave signaled a change. The foundation was now looking for hard-driving leaders, "a willingness to tackle some tough things with not a lot of road signs on how to do it," according to Martha Choe, its executive administrator. The foundation needed people comfortable with change. Most of those new hires would occupy the upper right quadrant. They were Explorers.

How do you manage such a shift in talent? For starters, it's extremely important simply to recognize it and to realize that the changes are bound to create tensions and casualties along the way. Plans to address these issues will differ from one company and one industry to the next.

Early on, the Gates Foundation tried team-building games, including a scavenger hunt around Seattle. That's a start. Another approach might be to promote or hire people who combine the two strengths, cultivating and exploring. They could serve as bridges between the two cultures, or flexors.

---

* https://archive.seattletimes.com/archive/?date=20061017&slug=gateshires17.

But perhaps the most effective strategy is to appeal to the shared mission. Practically everyone at the foundation could be making more money in the private sector. Yet a drive to battle disease throughout the world brought them to the non-profit. This was a purpose that appealed to Cultivators and Explorers alike. Both cultures would have to understand and accept the changes that were necessary for the mission.

David Cancel faced a different challenge in managing his engineers. A serial entrepreneur, Cancel is the founder and CEO of Drift, a messaging technology company in Cambridge, Massachusetts. He tells me that a lot of the best engineers are eager to fix problems and to innovate, but they tend to resent attempts to manage them. (I've experienced this firsthand.) Many of the engineers are patient, detail-oriented workers in the lower left Stabilizing quadrant. As they see it, the managers trying to corral them often don't truly understand the work they're doing. Consequently, communication between managers and these star engineers shrivels.

Cancel's talent design thinking innovation was to create a powerful new arm of management: the customers. Instead of having salespeople or the help desk deal with all the customer issues, he channeled some of that work to the engineering team. The customers had problems. The engineers helped fix them and, in the process, improved Drift's messaging product. The engineers were happy to work with far less interference from managers. All in all, a win-win.

STARTING WITH THE EXECUTIVE TEAM

Before launching a companywide initiative, it's often good to try out new approaches and ideas on the executive team. Talent design thinking is no exception. Change has to begin at the top.

We do this regularly at our company. As you can see in Figure 3.2, the largest number of us are in the upper right Explorer region.

FIGURE 3.2   The Predictive Index Executive Team CVF, with Mike Zani's and Daniel Musquiz's Dots Identified

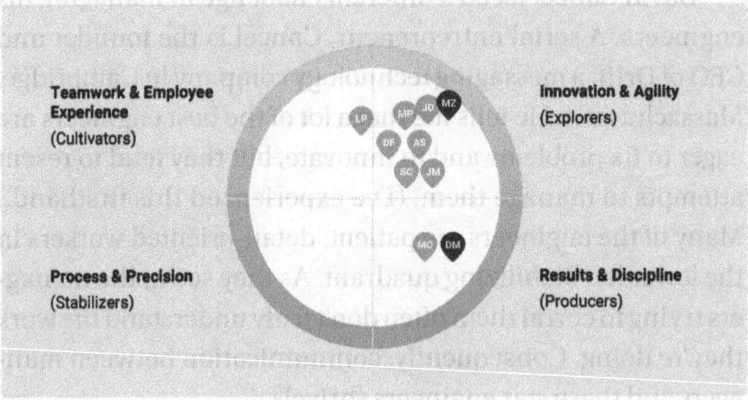

This is typical of a tech company in growth mode. The push is to expand into new markets, follow fresh ideas, and take chances. My business partner, Daniel, is in the Producer quadrant. He's more focused on the details of operations. Our head of client operations is a dyed-in-the-wool Producer: competitive, numbers-driven, and strategically focused.

This chart is pretty closely aligned with our strategy. This is to be expected, considering that talent optimization is our business. But this alignment is not forever. The world isn't static, and neither is a company's strategy. As startups grow, they often need to change their mix, focusing more on the nitty-gritty of productivity and quality control. And the economic climate imposes changes of its own. Coming out of the COVID-19 downturn, for example, many companies had to tweak their business plans. Such shifts require adjustments in talent.

BEYOND TALENT: ALIGNING IDEAS

If you ask everyone in the top ranks to answer the same strategy assessment, chances are that the results will be anything but uniform. When they take a close look, most companies find that they're misaligned, often badly. This means that not everyone follows the same priorities. Even if they agree on the end strategy, they're working at cross-purposes.

At first pass, the best companies—the top decile—are at 70 percent alignment. In other words, for every seven executives who are working in concert toward the strategic goals, three are fixed on other priorities. They're not all pulling in the same direction. Are you going to break ground on a house if you're only 70 percent aligned with the architect and contractor? Misalignment can sink everything from productivity to morale. And remember, 70 percent is the rate for the best companies. Most are much worse.

This comes as a shock to senior team members. Just the way a huge majority of drivers believe they're better than average, most executives believe that the company is aligned around the strategic goals as they see them. When this turns out not to be true, the CEO often shifts into head-hunting mode. Who's not aligned? (Who doesn't agree with me?)

The best approach, I've found, is to have everyone list the priorities as they see them. This can come from a standard list, like our strategy assessment, or people can come up with their own. A review of these priorities is bound to generate discussion. It's likely to be long and contentious. After all, people believe in their strategic visions, and are often passionate about initiatives that are viewed as nonstrategic, or even distractions. Sometimes, though, through discussion, they can change the consensus.

This alignment process can unearth all sorts of troubles within the company: hidden agendas, pet projects, personal rivalries. Certain team members might turn stubborn when hidden priorities start to emerge. If these dissenters fail to sell their plan or vision, they must climb onboard or move on. Otherwise, the company will still be misaligned.

Amazon founder Jeff Bezos addressed this issue in a 2017 letter to shareholders. His three-word command was "Disagree and Commit." "This phrase," Bezos wrote, "will save a lot of time. If you have conviction on a particular direction even though there's no consensus, it's helpful to say, 'Look, I know we disagree on this but will you gamble with me on it? Disagree and commit?' By the time you're at this point, no one can know the answer for sure, and you'll probably get a quick yes."

Bezos adds one important note. Sometimes it's the CEO who should disagree and commit. Alignment isn't always mandated from the top.

CHANGING THE DESIGN FOR GROWTH

Startups are laboratories for the kind of talent transformation we're discussing. They start out as loose confederations—groups of people, often friends—around the founder. In the beginning, there's no real design to it. There might be a technologist and maybe someone overseeing product, but most people are generalists. They do what has to be done, whether it's dealing with a needy customer or making a run for midnight pizza. Everyone reports to the CEO.

The company grows, and the CEO comes to an inevitable conclusion: he or she can't manage everybody. (In my experience, once you get more than eight direct reports, you either scrimp on necessary management or your head pops off.) The situation requires structure and levels. In the new scheme, a few people still report to the CEO, and others report to them.

This is where talent design thinking is crucial. If a growing company simply lets the structure evolve willy-nilly, it's bound to struggle. People won't know their roles, who their reports are, or even who they're working for. Information doesn't flow where it's needed. Companies that continue to grow with random structures are destined for management crisis and likely collapse.

Jim Alampi, a former executive and current management consultant, speaks incisively about this. He studies the crisis points that a company hits as it grows. He calls them "brick walls." They are tied not to revenue but instead to head count and the new complexity of managing a larger group. As a team expands, the management structure represents the biggest obstacle to growth.

The root of the problem, Alampi says, is an inability to delegate. The founding CEO, for example, seeing that the organization design of the company must evolve, hires someone to run the day-to-day operations of the company, or perhaps a sales manager. But this change in design must be accompanied by a change in behavior. The founder must hand over the work but often finds this difficult. "How do you let go?" Alampi asks. "How do you give up authority and control?"

Most companies never get past this choke point. Of all the US companies that file taxes, 94 percent have fewer than 10 employees. Of course, this includes many mom-and-pop businesses, from corner stores to Laundromats. But there are lots of other companies casting for venture funding. They may have big visions and talent, but when these companies grow beyond the seven or eight of the founding team, they hit the brick wall.

Some adjust and make it past this first barrier. By the time a company reaches a workforce of 25 to 40, departments start to form. The product person, who first handled it all by herself and then hired an assistant, now heads a product department. The same thing happens to engineering and maybe finance. These new department heads now find themselves with very different jobs. They're managing, with all the good and bad that comes with it. Naturally, this means they must focus on employee development, approving vacations and time off. They must hold their reports accountable for the quality of their work and deadlines.

As growth continues to 60 people, it's usually time to add another level. At this juncture, the CEO presides over a handful of vice presidents. Department heads, who report to them, manage the individual contributors.

This growth, while exciting, is inherently destabilizing. It changes people's jobs. And sometimes, you'll find, employees fail to grow as fast as the company. They're not in sync.

Consider the original team of eight that worked with the founder. As the company grows, this founding nucleus naturally advances. Some of them become department heads; others occupy the C-suite. But this change brings new complexity—budgets, timelines, strategic hiring—and not everyone in this original group thrives. "Jobs will always outgrow people," Alampi says. "The A or B player that you hired may become a C player as the company grows."

What this colleague needs, painful as it is to face, is a demotion (though it's a good idea to call it something less demeaning). This leads to an uncomfortable but necessary discussion. The goal is to work with such colleagues to find a graceful transition to a job in which they can thrive without suffering the humiliation of being bounced down two or three levels.

Occasionally, the challenge is the opposite. This occurs when the company isn't growing as fast as a star employee.

This might be someone who is ready for a big step up, maybe to run a division. But the company hasn't grown one yet. Again, it's time for a career talk. This is a star, and you have to find her a good career path. The design of the company might have to adjust to her, perhaps sprouting a new responsibility, maybe even a new division or management level. Otherwise, she's gone.

The other challenge at this point is to create a career path for the ground level of the org chart, the individual contributors who manage no one. All too often, they look around and see that the only path to success—power, recognition, and yes, money—is in management. When this happens, many of them will jostle to get onto the management track, even if they're not suited for it. Deep down, they might not want to manage people. They may prefer to work alone, in the patient and orderly realm of the lower left quadrant, the Stabilizers. Or maybe they're Cultivators, more comfortable working within a team than running one. Yet they're drawn to leadership because of a design flaw in the company: the only pathway up is through management.

That's why it's vital to create career tracks for individual contributors, along with metrics for gauging their success. This gives them a route to status, money, and more interesting projects. Most important, many of them are bound to be more productive—and happier—if they're not forced to compete for management jobs that don't suit them.

Whatever the workplace structure, it must always be malleable, a work in progress, because change is a constant. Talent shines brightest when deployed in a design that evolves with a company's strategic goals.

NEXT STEPS

- What is the company's mission? Circulate questionnaires about strategic priorities to senior executives to gauge their alignment (or lack thereof).
- If misaligned, meet to discuss where the differences are and how to close the gap.
- Have every employee, including members of the senior leadership team, take a psychometric assessment, either from PI or one of our competitors.
- Place the executive team's profiles within the CVF. You can do this automatically with PI software or by hiring a talent consultant.
- Analyze whether the group is oriented toward the strategic goals.
- Deploy the employee profiles, as dots, across a CVF.
- Analyze with the leadership team the alignment between your existing talent and the company's mission.

Fitting Talent to Strategy

Who runs your human resources strategy? Can you identify the person? In most companies, the answer to this question is, "Well . . ." After some thinking, executives can often point to a pocket of HR in sales, and maybe a few people who recruit and develop talent in manufacturing or production. Those managers need skills, and they go out and get them. Sometimes it works . . .

But HR strategy? In many places, it bounces up to the CEO, who usually lacks the time and expertise to focus on it.

To optimize a workforce and to align talent with strategy, it's essential to have someone on the team who is driven, or even obsessed, by the challenges and opportunities of maximizing talent. This person should also have strong management chops to mold and implement a plan. When facing crucial decisions about how to shape and position the employee base, even an inspired and tireless management team cannot afford to wing it.

Imagine a manufacturer, perhaps a steel company, that plans to invest $500 million in a new coating and finishing line. The goal is to plunge into the steel market for electric appliances, like washers and dryers. Now imagine that this company has no executive in charge of new technology. The CEO simply asks the marketing head and the chief financial officer to scout for the machinery. Maybe they should shop for it in Japan or Korea. They're not experts in tech, and it's not their job—yet the future of the company hinges on their efforts in this area.

That would be insane. The same holds true for human resources. As I've mentioned, the employees of most companies are by far their most important and expensive asset. So to recruit and manage the talent, especially through the kind of realignment we're discussing, a top-flight HR professional must be included in the highest tier of management.

Many companies wait way too long to hire an HR chief. This is understandable. If you're a 15-person startup, scratching and clawing to survive in a competitive niche, you're hoping with each precious hire to add production or boost revenue. It might be another coder or a star salesperson. An HR pro, by contrast, adds cost. With this person on board, are you better off next month or the following one? Probably not. So executives figure they can fill the post later—if at all.

I learned this firsthand a decade ago when I took the top job at Shape Up, a wellness startup that I had invested in and taken over from the two brilliant entrepreneurial doctors who had founded it. The company had nine people at the time. My first hire, without hesitation, was a talented and energetic VP of human resources, Jackie Dube. The founders were puzzled, and none too pleased. Why were we adding *overhead*, they asked, when we needed so much help in product development and sales?

It was true that we had only 10 people. But the plan was to grow that number to 50 over the next 12 months. "Ninety

percent of what I'm going to do is build a world-class team,"
I said. I asked Jackie to drown me in so much talent that
we could not help but crush our competition—and she did
just that.

Six years later, when Richard Branson's Virgin group
bought the much larger Shape Up, the company had thousands of corporate customers and 134 employees.

Most companies keep a flat organization in their early
years. The small team is composed of generalists, people who
can do lots of different jobs, whatever's needed. And they all
pitch in on HR, though it's no one's specialty. Then they start
to add some layers, as we saw in the previous chapter, maybe
hiring a VP for finance and another for sales. As a C-suite takes
shape, all kinds of questions emerge about spans of control
and reporting relationships. But it's usually not until the company grows to 100 people, or more, that CEOs look around and
decide they need someone to handle personnel—and wish
they'd thought about it sooner.

Even then, they often don't give the HR person much
power. The common mistake is to see it not as a strategic post,
but as a compliance job, with all those forms to fill out and
rules to follow. So they bring in a junior HR resource on the
cheap, and park this person with the finance team. Her job—
and it is often a her—is not to help transform the company. It's
largely to cross the t's, dot the i's, manage vacation accruals,
bonuses, and severance, run occasional workshops for sensitivity training or gender bias, and—above all—to oversee
compliance with state and federal regulations and to keep the
firm out of legal trouble.

It's only with an empowered HR strategist on board that
you can match your talent to your strategy. Perhaps you see
that you want to innovate and push into new markets, but it
turns out that most of your talent is in the Process & Precision quadrant, maximizing what you're already doing. Or

maybe you're shifting much of your business into virtual communications, and you need a host of people who know how to connect with others and create new types of teams. That would call for more Cultivating talent, from the upper left Teamwork & Employee Experience quadrant. How do you adjust your workforce?

I'd love to be able to give fail-safe guidance. If these misaligned assets were capital machinery or inventory, it wouldn't be so hard. But we're dealing with people with knowledge, who have relationships inside and outside of the company. It's complicated and hinges on the particulars of the company. Regardless of your approach, the process ahead is difficult, messy, and painful—but also necessary.

It comes down to four options:

1. **Hire and replace.** This can be brutal. It requires a delicate balance that Jim Collins, the author and management consultant, calls "rigorous and not ruthless." Nonetheless, it creates massive challenges in change management.

2. **Augment.** If you're lucky enough to be growing, you can bolster the talent in the areas needed by hiring, and easing those whose roles are no longer central along slower paths. The key is to augment with authority—and to keep the team from growing too large.

3. **Train to stretch.** This takes time. It is less disruptive, at least in the beginning, than replacement. It also sends a positive message that leadership is committed to investing in its workforce. The trouble is that when people are trained for a quadrant outside their comfort zone, they tend to be less efficient and find it less fulfilling. This can lead to frustration and acrimony.

None of these approaches is easy or painless. That's why a lot of companies turn to the next option, which often ends in failure.

4. **Muddling through.** This might mean replacing one person, demoting another, along with some retraining. The process involves understanding how much disruption the company can handle, and implementing at a scale and pace that brings about the change while maintaining productivity and a positive culture. Too often, though, muddling through is focused more on surviving today than winning tomorrow.

It's not an easy choice. Often the fate of the company hangs in the balance. So will it be hire and replace, a retraining regime, or a combination of the two?

The answer is usually determined by the time horizon. How quickly can you wait for the payback? How much time can you afford?

This is a common issue for sports franchises, from the Boston Red Sox to Manchester United. Is the strategy to win now, or to pursue lasting excellence? Those eager to win right away sign free agents, expensive veterans with a proven track record. That's hiring and replacing. Those with more patience invest their money in development, boosting their farm teams. This is parallel to a train and redeploy approach. Teams that sacrifice short-term success while developing talent enjoy the luxury of time, or at least believe they do. Either they have enough money to bankroll the down years, or they have a faithful and patient fan base who support them through thick and thin.

Like sports franchises, companies must base their restructuring strategies on their time horizon. Those that attempt to wrench themselves into alignment through training can afford to postpone a degree of productivity. Sometimes this comes from size. IBM, for example, runs an entire training academy. It has a big enough labor force to train at scale, hundreds at a time, without disrupting the work of the rest.

Family-run companies can often afford a longer time horizon than others. They're naturally loath to fire sons, daughters, and cousins. And if they're not in a rapidly evolving cutthroat industry, they can get by for a few years while retraining. The investors, being family, are patient, and the workers, in the best case, are committed to the company and ready to adapt to its needs.

These are the exceptions. While training remains an important element, most companies don't have time to transform through training. It's too slow.

This is especially true for enterprises backed by private equity, with its focus on return on investment. For leaders of such companies, time is money, and they're usually eager to spend early and get their return. They're often happy to explore the free-agent market. So they retain headhunters and prepare to pay hefty compensation.

Even startups without private equity investors feel the pressure to move fast. Most of them, after all, eventually fail or are consumed. With this focus on survival, most can ill afford to hobble along though a multiyear transition, underperforming. If they get overtaken in their market, they may never catch up. It's this scarcity of time that discourages many from an intense retraining strategy. They feel they don't have slack for it. After all, you can borrow or raise money for a hiring binge, but you can't borrow or raise time.

Bowing to the dictates of the calendar and of investors eager for rising numbers every quarter, they change largely by hiring and replacing.

This has been the case in every company we've bought. Before buying The Predictive Index, we looked at each one as a five-year turnaround project. In each company, the established workforce was woefully misaligned with our growth strategy, so we used the hiring and replacing approach.

These changes are easier when a new management team comes in. This was the case when we bought The Predictive Index in 2014. It was a 60-year-old company that was run by a trustee. It was fine-tuned to provide a steady stream of revenue for the family. The strategy, in essence, was to stick to the same routines and not to rock the boat.

We had a starkly different strategy. It was to grow dramatically, and to position The Predictive Index at the heart of the nascent talent optimization industry. That was the vision we had sold to our investors. To put it in the terms of the Competing Values Framework, we needed a team heavily tilted toward the upper right quadrant, Explorers who would not only plow into new markets but also dream them up.

What we found, by contrast, were 34 people who had been diligently implementing assessments and services conceived six decades earlier. Some fit into Cultivating, many had the detailed focus of Stabilizing, and a few, especially in sales, populated the Producing, or Results & Discipline quadrant. But the upper-right Innovation & Agility quadrant was virtually empty. We were short on Explorers. While we had arrived ready and eager to take risks, our workforce was risk averse.

We knew that we'd be hiring and replacing. But it couldn't be immediate. That wouldn't be fair to the employees, and in the short term, we needed them to keep running the company and servicing customers.

It was a delicate process. The first step in our transition, in every company we've taken over, has been communication. We don't want to surprise anybody, and it's important that employees know and understand the change ahead. We also made it clear that we were kicking off a cultural change based on clear communications and high performance. It would take years, but the seeds were sown on that first day.

We started with the Why. We explained what wasn't working and where we were planning to go. We told them that we'd be counting on their readiness and ability to change and their buy-in on the strategy. We let them know that for many, this process would be uncomfortable, and that some of them would likely prefer to leave for other opportunities.

Throughout the process of change management, discomfort is crucial, and taking refuge in the old status quo must be impossible. The model for this management of discomfort is the Spanish conquistador Hernán Cortés. In 1519, when he and his soldiers landed on Mexico's mosquito-infested coast near Veracruz, he ordered his soldiers to burn the ships that brought them there. His strategy—to call it "uncomfortable" would be a dramatic understatement—was to march inland through an unknown land and conquer an empire. He knew that the temptation would be to turn back and sail home. That no longer was an option.

We jokingly call my partner, Daniel, our Chief Discomfort Officer. He works to make the status quo so uncomfortable that change is the more appealing option. He introduces discomfort at every step.

"We've always done it this way," he hears.

"From now on, we're doing it this other way," he says.

"But that's harder."

"Right." And he explains why it's necessary.

Sometimes he takes away a favorite tool or procedure, one that anchors people to the old way of doing business. More discomfort.

At this point, a few people come forward, usually quietly, and whisper that they actually like the new approach better. They were waiting for change, feeling stultified, and they're happy to see new ideas and strategies. Those employees, chances are, will be sticking around, at least for a while.

Others complain. As I see it, the response to wrenching realignment breaks down somewhere around 20/20/60. Some 20 percent of the people embrace change, and an equal number reject it. The goal is to sell it to the 60 percent in the middle.

To guide the analysis, I used to keep a sheet of paper folded up in my wallet (see list on page 64). It contained a long list of skills divided into three columns: those that are easy to change, harder but doable, and nearly impossible to develop. For example, it's relatively easy to change customer focus, goal setting, or running meetings. It's harder, but far from impossible, to develop team skills in an employee, to help the person become more likeable or a strategic thinker. But when it comes to boosting an employee's intelligence, creativity, tenacity, or integrity, it's hardly worth trying.

For those who appear to be struggling to fit in the new regime, it might be time for a serious talk. We want you to be an A player, we say. Can we augment what you're doing to make you one? Are there other roles that might work for you in the new scheme? Are you willing to change?

If the answers are no, no, and no, the path is quite clear. The next stop for these employees is what we call Happy Alumni. I'll cover this in more depth in Chapter 6. The essence is that we want to help them in every way we can, from lining them up for other opportunities to providing generous severance. Though often painful, this transition should lead to a better situation for them and for us. Maybe our paths will cross again. But they're leaving.

In many cases, the signals aren't quite so clear. People say they're ready to change, and they make the effort, but the results are so-so. These employees cannot continue this way. What they need is another dose of discomfort. This sounds mean. But it boils down to pushing them harder, so that they either up their game or decide that it's not for them. The goal, after all, is to put every employee in a position to thrive, inside the company or elsewhere. So-so work isn't fulfilling for anyone.

Meanwhile, we're adding people who fit into our strategy. These are strong performers who will push the company ahead where it's weak. We can't change the direction of the company with a symbolic hire or two. We need numbers of impact players.

At this point, legacy employees often find themselves bumped down a level in the org chart. Maybe they used to report to the president, and now they report to this new person, who might be in a different office 1,000 miles away. That's more discomfort. A few more people inquire about severance packages.

The way I'm describing it, Daniel and I sound like Grim Reapers. I know this. And if you look at the numbers, it's true. The survival rates at companies we take over are in the single digits within a few years. It happens every time. During this process, getting rid of underperforming employees— what I call C and D players—is usually not so hard. They sense clearly that they'd be happier and more productive elsewhere.

One obstacle might arise, though. Let's say you have a C player handing a necessary job, and you haven't found a replacement yet. Should you keep the employee on the job longer? The answer is probably no. As consultant Jim Alampi suggests, open up that space and let other people take over the duties on a provisional basis. There's a good chance the A players were wondering what was taking you so long.

But the workplace doesn't have to feel so grim during this winnowing. In fact, it can't—because success is predicated on people working together with common purpose and enjoying it. This is central to the cultural challenge companies face, which I'll cover in the next chapter.

Still, there is one scenario during these transitions that makes me feel absolutely awful. It involves the B+ employee. This is a person who embraces the change, takes on the discomforts, supports the colleagues and the mission, and yet . . . fails to produce consistent top-quality results.

The question of what to do with a B+ worker can keep me up at night. It's a bit like romantic relationships that seem destined for marriage, but then fall short. Those are painful breakups because so much value, effort, and hope has been invested into them.

Connections to the B+ worker can be very strong and hard to sever. Sometimes a heart-to-heart talk can solve the issue. The employee agrees to take another position; maybe you take something off their plate to reduce complexity. But sometimes there's no clear path within the company. It can be excruciating to send the B+ employee toward alumni status. The goal is to give them as much support as possible, along whichever path.

Then there are the cases of dissenters. The people working in our distribution channels had been on the job for decades, and had developed their routines long before the age of the internet. They labored with pencil and paper, and they believed they knew the company far better than these new guys who had just bought it.

Thinking schematically, as I've mentioned, there's likely a group, around 20 percent, that resists. Among them, there might be a few active dissenters. Here, it is sometimes necessary to crack down and publicly admonish an active malcontent. This sends a signal to everyone else that the new direction is established, and no longer a matter of debate. It paves the way for greater alignment, some of it from new talent and some from old.

STRATIFIED SYSTEMS THEORY

What do you have to do next week? What will be on your plate four months from now? How about in two years? If you pose these questions to different people in your organization, you're sure to get very different answers. Some will provide full to-do lists for different scenarios, while others will shrug, wondering why you're asking questions that seem irrelevant to their jobs.

People across an enterprise hold wildly different ideas about the future. During the Cold War, a psychologist named Elliott Jaques carried out research on this subject and called it the Stratified Systems Theory. The idea, which was especially useful for the military, is that different jobs require different time horizons. Certain people are comfortable projecting far into the future, while others limit their view to a single week, or even a day. So the trick for a large bureaucracy, Jaques wrote, was to layer the talent according to people's time horizons.*

If that sounds a tad theoretical, consider concrete examples. An engineer is heading up a team building a manufacturing plant. Working on the construction might be a welder who handles assignments thrown his way. He doesn't have to plan too much for tomorrow or the next day. His time horizon can be counted in hours.

But the engineer takes a longer view. He has to consider the supplies he'll need next month and the month after. By that point, winter storms might be blowing through. How will that affect supply chains and construction? He's dealing with a number of variables over a time frame of several months. Next year, he knows, he'll have a different project. But he doesn't have to plan for it.

---

* https://apps.dtic.mil/dtic/tr/fulltext/u2/a298621.pdf.

His boss does. She's a regional manager who has financial responsibilities, a profit and loss report due every quarter. She's already prospecting for next year's projects, some of them in Europe. She's busy calculating how many workers she'll need, considering currency hedges, and gauging the risk of banking on contract laborers, which hinges on the job market next spring. She has to think ahead, at least a year or two.

She reports to a chief executive, who might be plotting an Asian strategy, including a massive acquisition in Japan. This person has to weigh variables far into the future, perhaps a decade, even longer.

When Elliott Jaques was drawing up his Stratified Systems Theory for the military, the expanding time frames, Strata 1 through 5 (see Figure 4.1), fit neatly into a rigid hierarchy. Privates didn't need to think about the future, only to follow orders hour by hour. Each ascending rank required a longer vision, until you got to five-star generals, who had to consider the geopolitical implications in 5 years, or 10, of nuclear weapons development or the containment strategy of the Soviet Union.

FIGURE 4.1 Expanding Time Frames in Stratified Systems Theory

Strata	Learning & Problem Solving Modes	Longest Time Span "Planning"	Role	Measurement
5	Synthesizing Data Prediction/Forecasting	5+ years	Goal, vision & macro strategy development	Entire System Success
4	Modeling Scenarios Using "If, Then Analysis"	2–4 years	Multisystems or department integration	Integrated System Output
3	Analysis–Drive Toward Cause & Effect	9–18 months	System design	Predictability of Work
2	Experience/History They "Weighs Options"	3–9 months	Schedule the work & make sure the work gets done	Accuracy, Completeness, Timeliness
1	Doing–Trial and Error	1 day–1 month	Work/production/output	Quality, Speed

This table is based on the works of Ellliott Jaques and Tom Foster.

While few of us run companies as hierarchically rigid as the military, it's still valuable to measure the time horizons that employees are comfortable with, and to use them in the deployment of talent.

There are tremendous advantages in a workforce marked by higher strata proficiency. We strive for it in our company. One big plus is that a person who envisions what's ahead is more likely to figure out what to do—thinking through the steps that lead in the right direction. These people need less management, and are frequently self-starters. They're more likely to generate ideas because they're imagining the future and scenario planning. People who think far ahead also have potential to climb into management and executive roles.

Getting a grip on strata is fundamental for designing reporting relationships in an enterprise. Think of what happens, for example, if a chief executive has an administrative assistant who functions on a Strata 1 level. To manage this person, the CEO must drop down to Strata 2, allocating perhaps 15 minutes every morning to go over what the assistant is going to do and how to handle certain calls and emails and calendar items. This is not time well spent. And for this reason, many CEOs hire executive assistants who function at high strata levels. These elite assistants can see the entire operation, and anticipate what's ahead and what needs to be done. Often, they shed the assistant moniker and become executives in their own right.

If you're in a small startup, you don't need to think much about reporting relationships. But as a company grows to 200 people, it develops new levels, with executive vice presidents and division leaders. It's while managing talent in such an enterprise, with five or six levels, that the strata take on importance. Ideally, each level will have to drop only one strata to manage its reports. Big gaps waste time and lead to frustration.

How do you test for strata? Tom Foster, a management consultant and author, proposes a question, such as: "When you finish what you're working on now, how do you get more work?" Some people say they wait for their next assignment. Others ask their manager. Others might start to enumerate everything they know that needs to get done. The answer often reveals a person's time horizon.

I often test for strata during the hiring process. After all, if we want high-strata employees, the job interview is a great place to screen for it. I might ask candidates to tell me a story about the most complicated project they ever undertook in their youth or early in their career. I'm not looking for altruism or team play or any other virtues. I'm focused on comfort with complexity and long-span thinking.

Some people, eager to flash their entrepreneurial credentials, tell me about a business they started. But when you poke further, there's little there. For example, someone designs a website in college. It's pretty good. And a local business pays him $500 to make another one. Pretty soon, he has a small business of his own, which pays a chunk of his expenses through college. That's great, but it doesn't show strategic vision.

One of the best strata stories I heard was from a former high school actor named Rich Weiss. He and his friend worked on sets for a high school play. That didn't sound so complicated to me at first. But then he described the constraints. There wasn't much money or space. They had to figure out how to make a set that fit into the gym, one the school used for all kinds of activities. So the set had to be compact, moveable, and affordable. They had to plan in September to build it over the winter holidays, without interfering with basketball and gymnastics, and then stage it in March. Rich was clearly a strategic thinker. He now uses those skills to run important processes at our company. He doesn't have to wait around for someone to tell him what needs to be done.

50 CRUCIAL COMPETENCIES

For the "relatively easy to change" and the "harder but do-able" columns, coaching can help. The "very difficult to change" list is best addressed through proper hiring.

Relatively Easy to Change	Harder but Do-able	Very Difficult to Change
Risk taking	Judgment	Intelligence
Leading edge	Strategic skills	Analysis skills
Education	Pragmatism	Creativity
Experience	Track record	Conceptual ability
Organization/planning	Resourcefulness	Integrity
Self-awareness	Excellence standards	Assertiveness
Communication-oral	Independence	Inspiring followership
Communications-written	Stress management	Energy
First impression	Adaptability	Passion
Customer focus	Likability	Ambition
Political savvy	Listening	Tenacity
Selecting A players	Team player	
Redeploying B/C players	Negotiation skills	
Coaching/training	Persuasiveness	
Goal setting	Team builder	
Empowerment	Change leadership	
Performance management	Inclusivity (diversity)	
Running meetings	Conflict management	
Compatibility of needs	Credible vision	
	Balance in life	

NEXT STEPS

- Identify who runs strategic HR in your organization. Possibly, your head of sales is good at it, or your head of technology. They are usually responsible for their teams, and the good ones get it. (If you cannot identify the person, then it is *you*, and it's not likely your specialty.)
- If you manage just one person, you need a talent strategy, even if it is simplistic. So hire (or promote) a strategic HR person, one who is committed to HR's key role in strategy.
- Identify your C and D players and discuss their potential. Give each manager a maximum of one turnaround project.

The Cultural Imperative

I was an avid sea dog in high school and climbed high in the national rankings as a competitive sailor. So naturally, I was thrilled to be accepted into the class of 1992 at the Naval Academy at Annapolis, Maryland. It seemed like the perfect fit.

Upon arriving in Annapolis, my classmates and I endured Plebe Summer. Early on, they shaved our heads and took our clothes, and while we went through exhausting physical tests, they ignored our names and called us Plebes. The idea was to suppress our individuality and break us down. Eventually, we could earn back our identities, but only within the Navy's culture.

In the military, cultural identity is intentional, defined, preached, and policed. Creating and maintaining a strong culture is crucial to its mission.

Each branch, I learned, has a different flavor. The Marines are the first ones in. Their culture revolves around Mission Accomplished. This is drilled in from day one at boot camp, and it's intense. Marines reinforce the lessons with pain and with shame. It's an ordeal and involves sacrifice. But in return, Marines gain trust in each other, consistency, and reliability. The culture is central to their warrior ethos.

The Army is a bit more like a corporation. It has diversity and lots of different modes of operation. It masters logistics and scale, and it must be more strategic. The Air Force pushes mastery of technology and speed. In the Navy, the ship itself is, in effect, a central member of the team, and everyone's welfare hinges upon keeping the ship fit and afloat. The culture supports that mission.

Every culture, whether it's the Marines, the Catholic Church, or a machine shop in Missouri, has its strengths and vulnerabilities, even its dysfunctions. The military cultures, for example, are fabulous for discipline. To this end, they discourage individualism and remain largely closed to ideas and flows of information from below. Consequently, they can miss out on insights and creativity. They also tend to frustrate assertive and independent types like me. (I transferred to Brown after my first year at Annapolis).

The important lesson to be learned from the military is not the secret of one successful culture or another, but instead the idea that molding a culture is the starting point for each enterprise. The central challenge for all of us in business is to pursue this proactively, to create a culture that supports the mission. This doesn't just happen. It takes an ongoing effort.

Many enterprises don't dwell much on culture. The founder or CEO, if asked about the culture, will often say that it's good, which means that it's a place that is comfortable for him (and it's usually a him). He works the way he wants, and hires people who appear to be on the same wavelength. Some people fall by the wayside and go elsewhere. They don't fit.

Then something happens. A rock star in the sales department bothers colleagues with dirty or sexist jokes. Top managers carry out business over a closed poker game. To meet stretch targets, plant managers start shipping defective units.

It's when crises emerge that the CEO is forced to confront crucial questions about whatever culture has taken root in the enterprise, and whether the executive team should take steps to change it.

The key for each company is to settle on the appropriate culture much earlier, ideally from the start. It should be designed and maintained intentionally to attract the right talent and fit the mission. It is upon the foundation of a strong and defined culture, as we'll see, that dream teams are built.

READING REPORT CARDS

For many companies, the first step toward establishing a winning culture is to figure out what's already in place. Thankfully, this is a lot easier than it used to be because employees, both current and former, are talking about it every day and sharing their thoughts online.

At the dawn of the public internet, even while most people struggled with slow dial-up connections, it was quickly apparent that employees had gained new ways to communicate outside their company walls and tell the whole world what life was like in their company. One popular site during the dot-com era was called FuckedCompany.com. It was nasty, as the name suggests, and open to abuse. But it delivered the goods. Companies panned on that site soon found it was much harder to attract top talent, or that they had to pay more for it.

Today, sites like Glassdoor, kununu, and Blind provide a much broader range of services, with more science and data, and less attitude. These networked services provide an always updated report card on each company's culture, as experienced by employees. This is fundamental intelligence for HR.

The rankings on these sites are as simple as can be, much like the restaurant review site Yelp. Companies that make people feel good about their jobs and appear to respect them get high ratings, over four stars. The bad ones get fewer.

Now you might check out some companies online and find some low-ranking successes—companies whose rotten rankings haven't interfered with earnings growth or a high-flying stock. Some of them can no doubt make a case that their punishing model works. If a company has a winning algorithm, a breakthrough drug on patent, or a gold-plated roster of long-time customers, it can thrive despite a toxic culture of fear, secrecy, and backstabbing.

Indeed, this has been a model, especially for turnaround champions. One of the most celebrated, Albert "Chainsaw Al" Dunlop, managed to cut costs and goose earnings while eviscerating workforces at Campbell's Soup and Sunbeam. Dunlap, also known as "Rambo in Pinstripes," once posed for a magazine cover wearing an ammo belt across his chest. Any success he had (before his fall for fraudulent accounting at Sunbeam) was mostly about lowering costs, not optimizing employee fit and satisfaction. Dream teams weren't part of his strategy or culture.

The cultures I'm describing are the polar opposite of what Chainsaw Al built. They require harmony and trust. They thrive on rich flows of information. People must feel free to express their ideas and concerns. That's how the enterprise, with its collective intelligence, grows smarter.

To pursue this mode, and to attract and maintain top talent, no company can afford to have ratings in the lower half. This is because the star performers have choices. And why would they go to a company with a loser ranking? (When was the last time you went to a restaurant with an abysmal rating on Yelp?) Maybe if it offers a premium salary, a few will sign on. But if the workplace turns out to be as poisonous as advertised, they'll be on their way in no time.

So you've got to rank in the top half, scoring at least 3.5 out of 5. How to get there? First things first. If the toxic culture comes from top management, there's little chance the chief executive will want to fix it, or even see anything wrong. In those cases, you can only hope that the board picks up on it and replaces the leadership. Decapitation is the quickest answer for a toxic culture at the top.

For everyone else, the first step is to carry out research. This means reading the reviews on websites and, importantly, gathering data from your own employees.

The best place to start is by measuring the magic at the heart of a healthy and productive workplace: engagement. When we're engaged, our minds are entirely focused on our work.

Think about a miserable customer experience you've had. You ask someone for help, whether it's an insurance company or the grocery store. The person shrugs and tells you to ask someone else: it's not their job to respond. Technically, maybe these people are right. They don't "have to" help. But they're also telling you loud and clear that they won't lift a finger to do anything beyond their job description, and they don't seem to care what you think.

The crucial difference between the "have to" and "want to" workers is discretionary effort. Looking at the chart in Figure 5.1, you can see that early on in the process, the two lines both advance. The "want to" workers advance, naturally, but the "have to" also improve, though from a lower floor. The difference in the trajectories takes place at the moment the "have to" workers reach the comfy plateau of "minimum requirements." That's where they remain while the others keep improving.

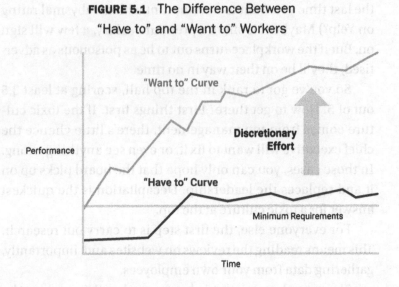

FIGURE 5.1 The Difference Between "Have to" and "Want to" Workers

Disengagement doesn't merely pollute much of the labor economy. Sadly, it defines it. Gallup's 2019 State of the Global Workplace study found that approximately 85 percent of workers are "not engaged" on the job. They're cognitively disconnected, emotionally uninvested, and unfulfilled. This is a sad conclusion because people who are disengaged are unproductive and, more often than not, unhappy. And that unhappiness doesn't go poof! the minute they leave work. It's all too likely to darken their home life as well.

Employees who do only what's absolutely necessary are poisonous for morale, customer satisfaction, and productivity. They usually are not engaged.

Indeed, between the "Have to" and the "Want to" curves lies a vast cultural chasm. For those who work because they want to and are fully engaged, the hours whiz by, virtually unnoticed. Engaged workers stretch beyond, sometimes far beyond, what they're supposed to do. This discretionary effort is worth gold. This is the stuff dream teams are made of.

Fortunately, engagement happens to be easy to measure and to track. At our company, we do it with an employee experience assessment. It takes about 15 minutes and features 80 questions. Most of them are straightforward. It asks employees, for example, to rank the degree to which "My manager brings out the best in people," or "The people I work with take the time to understand each other's point of view."

To get the best information, trust is essential. If this doesn't exist, you'll have to guarantee anonymity. That produces far less valuable data because, while you can draw conclusions about the team and the manager, you lose sight of the individual employee. If you have built a strong foundation of trust, however, and if the employees believe that the goal of the survey is to help them thrive, you can shift from completely anonymous to confidential non-anonymous. With that, the engagement of each individual comes into clear focus.

We use one fourth of their answers to measure engagement: how much of their time, energy, and ideas flow into the job. The other three-quarters provide context. In cases where engagement is low, they point to the root of the problem, the disconnect. It might be the company itself, a person not aligned with its mission or its culture, the manager or the team, or the job itself. If employees have the confidence that honest answers won't get them into trouble, they deliver this intelligence.

THE PLATINUM RULE

In a sense, a company is like an intelligent machine. It comes up with answers. It solves problems. It innovates. And its collective strength is that each person knows and sees things that others miss. Drift's David Cancel regards each person's input as vital feedback loops. "You can't be afraid to open up to the good, the bad, and the ugly," he says. This intelligence is vital for a company to correct its course.

A key to a healthy culture is the freedom to make mistakes and admit them. Yuchun Lee, a serial entrepreneur in Boston, says he spends an hour with new hires to introduce them to the culture he's building. It's one in which every mistake is a learning opportunity. "You need to take the leap of faith," he says, "that if you accept your mistakes, you'll advance faster." He would be "terrified," he adds, if people expected him to be right 100 percent of the time. "About 15 percent of what I say is going to be wrong," he tells colleagues. "Tell me which 15 percent."

In a toxic environment, trust is too scarce to admit mistakes or discontent, or even to answer a questionnaire honestly. There's often an assumption that if an employee is unhappy, it's that person's fault, so it's natural to cover it up. In such a workplace, workers are expected to bend to the norms and dictates of the company, the manager, and the team—or at least to pretend they do.

Our approach turns this notion on its head. The manager's job is not to fit each employee into a box. It's not even to follow the Golden Rule and manage each team member as the boss herself would want to be managed. No, the goal is to follow the Platinum Rule, to treat people the way *they* want to be treated. This involves getting to know them, how they like to work, collaborate, and consume information, how and where they find purpose and fulfillment.

Many assume that engagement is tied to salary or benefits. This is not the case. We've found that for employees to feel OK about their jobs, compensation must fall within the ballpark of what they would make elsewhere. If they find out that they're making significantly less, they can feel exploited. Morale takes a hit, and engagement can fall. However, payment above the industry norm does not lift engagement.

The secret to stoking engagement is to answer, convincingly, the big Why. Why are we doing this work? Is it, like Tesla, to accelerate the advent of sustainable transit? Maybe for a production company, it's to create the funniest TV series ever, or in the case of a fire department, to serve the community by protecting lives and property. In some businesses, it's simply to make money. (Hey, it's better not to pretend otherwise.)

Not everyone will buy into the Why, no matter how compelling it may seem. A certain number will scoff at the mission statement and grumble about corporate retreats. (A far larger number will roll their eyes when handed T-shirts or hats emblazoned with feel-good slogans.) This skepticism is to be expected.

It's crucial, though, to have a core of respected employees who embrace the mission and make the discretionary effort again and again. In successful cultures, these people are respected, and they set the norm. If there are too few, the engaged workers look like outliers. The skeptics see them as maniacs or, worse, brownnosers. There has to be a critical mass, a large enough contingent, to infect the entire herd with enthusiasm.

Conversely, toxic environments can export their poison. Lee, the entrepreneur, says that he shies away from hiring people from companies with low scores on sites like Glassdoor. "The baggage comes with them, and the old mental model," he says. Worse, they tend to hire people who respond to the same culture of secrecy and fear. It's like a contagion.

When I encounter successful cultures, I feel like hiring people right away. I've seen salespeople at Apple Stores and at Costco who go to extraordinary lengths to serve a customer. I've offered such people jobs. They almost always say no because they're fully engaged where they are.

Engagement is not only pixie dust for productivity. It's also glue. The most engaged employees tend to stick around.

LISTENING TO THE STARS

Let's say that the engagement surveys come back, and they point to a problem with a manager. Five of seven people on his team point to issues.

What to do? It's pretty simple. You present the manager with the scores and make it clear that he must turn around the disengagement. His first step is to meet with the team, both as a group and individually. They're the ones who can teach him how to manage them. So he lays his cards on the table and makes himself vulnerable. This is not a lot of fun. He tells them he's getting bad scores and is determined to do better. He asks, what's wrong, and how can we fix it? The first meeting should be with the team, followed by sit-downs with each individual.

While it's great to be open and vulnerable, and to listen, that doesn't mean that the manager should accept at face value all the criticism from disengaged employees. They're not always right.

Not long ago, for example, we went through a bunch of assessments and found out that a significant number of people said that we were moving too fast. It was unsettling for them. When we did an analysis, almost all of those who made this complaint scored in the bottom half on performance.

A much smaller number of people, we found, were making the opposite complaint, insisting that we should turbocharge our efforts and move much faster. These people, it turned out, were our engaged superstars. They were the ones we listened to.

We also pay attention, as you might expect, to psychometric assessments. They can help spot likely sources of friction in the management chain—and point out how to eliminate them.

Here's an example: If you look at my profile, whether in Myers-Briggs or PI, and compare it to the software developers down the hall, we look like different species. I'm in a hurry, and I have high dominance, which means that I prefer things done my way. The developers, on the other hand, are extremely patient and meticulous, and thankfully, most of them are fully engaged in their work. They want the time to get the code just right—and don't need an impatient CEO sticking his head in their area on a regular basis and asking for progress reports.

We're a bad mix. This came through loud and clear on the engagement surveys. So I put a person in between us who's a better match for their personalities and style of work. They don't see nearly as much of me as they used to, and they're happy about that.

ASKING SIMPLE QUESTIONS

It's amazing how much information you can gather about performance just by asking the employees. One time we added a single request to the engagement survey: List 10 people not in your department who make outstanding contributions to the company.

From this simple question, which cost no money, we received loads of valuable insights. Coworkers know better than anyone who the stars are. There were people who worked in the deepest bowels of the tech department, who rarely ventured out into the day, who got tremendous scores.

People know. It's just a question of asking them. And when you can honor the great work done by these people, it boosts morale and the culture of excellence.

But you can hit speed bumps. We have. You might think that a nimble and responsive enterprise would gather data quickly and reward stars by giving them prompt promotions. And that no doubt was true a decade or two ago. However, today's younger workforce is also focused on fairness and everybody getting a chance.

Three-quarters of our employees are in their twenties or thirties. When we gave one of them a rapid and well-deserved promotion, there was an outcry. It wasn't fair, we were told, because some people might have been on vacation or otherwise out of the loop during that week. They didn't have a chance to make their bid for the job.

Young people today operate in a world in which some of the most powerful CEOs on the planet are their age. Many of them view the slow-climbing career paths in Fortune 500 companies as relics. If there's an opportunity, no matter how lofty, many of them want a shot.

So, if a small group of the executive team agrees that a rising star deserves a big job, my advice is to take a minute to think about how others might feel—and adjust the steps and timetable to give them a shot.

CHANGING COURSE

Change happens. A culture that sped the company through unbridled growth in its early days suddenly confronts new challenges, ones that accompany success. There might be political and regulatory issues, customer lawsuits, or bad press, and the culture has to adapt to this new environment.

Meghan Joyce, a talented executive, experienced this process at Uber. Joyce, following a stint of crisis control at the US Treasury after the 2008 market crash, took a top job at Uber. When she joined, Uber was a raging startup with stratospheric ambition. It wanted to remake the way people move in cities, leading automobile transportation into the networked age and, eventually, to automation. At this stage, CEO Travis Kalanick had made a name for himself by defying local authorities and taxi unions. His strategy was to disrupt first, and answer questions later. This meant unleashing the network without asking for permission and gaining millions of satisfied customers. Then, strengthened by public support and a fast-climbing market valuation in the billions, Uber could confront the regulators from a position of power.

During this period, Joyce says, the company was highly decentralized. She was general manager in Boston, and it was up to her to respond to challenges. "They'd say, 'Here's a promo code. Sign up as many drivers as you can. We'll see in an hour and a half how well you did.'" Managers were encouraged to innovate and try stuff out. In the traditional balance between freedom and control, this was freedom turned up to 11.

The hiring protocol reflected this. The focus was capability. Job applicants' first step was a three-hour Excel-based analytics test. "We needed our team to be highly self-sufficient," Joyce says. "You were making decisions about your P&L on a daily basis." The culture was to "step on toes, charge through walls," which is great for growth, but not for building a sustainable enterprise.

This became clear when Uber got into trouble. By 2017, regulators and city officials were clamping down, threatening to block the rideshare giant. It also surfaced that Uber had built software called Greyball into its app expressly to deceive regulators. Meanwhile, newspapers began reporting on elements of a toxic workplace culture, including accounts of groping, sexual harassment, homophobic slurs, even an unhappy manager who reportedly threatened to knock the head of an underperforming employee with a baseball bat.*

The company's reputation was in freefall. In June 2017, the board pushed out the founding CEO, and in August it replaced him with Dara Khosrowshahi, who had a much quieter and more accommodating style.

---

* https://www.nytimes.com/2017/02/22/technology/uber-workplace-culture.html.

If Uber was going to survive, it would need to change its original culture, Joyce said. "We had to move from entrepreneurial and decentralized, and make way for a culture tilted toward compliance." This meant shifting the model from a hub and spokes org chart to a matrix. To exert control over the company, information had to flow in different channels. As part of this change, the regional managers no longer ran their own P&Ls.

Uber had to shift its focus toward compliance. The company couldn't forget about growth and numbers, of course. But they had to grapple with a new question. "What does good look like from a compliance perspective?"

To push this cultural shift, Uber began to hire differently and bring on board different types of employees—people who were strong on rules and reputation management. In our framework, Uber stopped focusing entirely on the extroverted right side of the chart, where the Explorers and Producers rule the roost, and looked for Stabilizers, from the lower-left Process & Precision quadrant. These people tend to be more patient, and they hew to the rules.

For Uber, this cultural pivot may have saved the company.

CULTURAL ADAPTATION

Sometimes, a new CEO or a new owner comes in, and a culture gap emerges. I've seen this happen up close.

In 2009, Daniel and I had carried out the turnaround of our small manufacturer outside Detroit, LEDCO. Productivity and profits were up dramatically, in large part because we had a high-performing team. We'd pushed responsibility for decision-making and budgets down into the organization. Teams had broad autonomy to innovate. Communication was fluid. In short, it was the original test case—and template—for the talent optimization I'm writing about in this book.

But Daniel and I weren't going to stick with LEDCO forever. When an offer to buy came in, we sold. This plunged the company into dramatic cultural change.

The new owners, leaders of a company called Havis, Inc., had a history of success—and their own ideas about how to operate that was totally different from ours. The CEO wanted to run things from the top down. Our methods sounded to him like a lot of what he would call hoity-toity business-school thinking. He kept his own counsel and made calculations on the back of envelopes. He smoked, and consequently, smokers got more CEO access.

I was still around, helping manage the transition. But after six months, I went to him and told him to run it his way. It didn't make any sense to try to stitch the two cultures together.

Despite all the change, the company remained profitable. Smart managers can find all kinds of ways to win. But the company lost a lot of great people. They didn't fit anymore.

A few of them knocked on our doors. That's one advantage of building a culture geared toward open communication and engagement. Talent flocks to it.

DEFINING VALUES

In the early days after we bought The Predictive Index, Daniel and I hired the same talented HR consultant I'd worked with at Shape Up, Jackie Dube. We were racing into a hiring mode, so she sat us down and asked us what kind of culture we wanted to build.

You can imagine what followed. We went on and on, listing adjectives for our dream workforce. We wanted self-starters, honest communicators, and team players. We wanted smarts and speed, of course, but not prima donnas.

After our first session, we had a wish list that would have described half to two-thirds of the startups in the world. Everyone wants stars. But how to mold that wish list into something that would express the values of the enterprise we hoped to build? This effort clearly needed more work because what would set us apart and define our culture had more to do with values and attitudes than skills and best practices.

Our goal was to have a set of values, ideally expressed in an acronym, that we could share with employees and recruits. It would communicate the quid pro quo. Here's what you're joining. Here's what you get, and here's what's expected of you.

Coming up with such a manifesto takes a while. It takes even longer to wring out the clichés and create a list that feels authentic, something everyone can rally around.

We drew up a draft. It included values like teamwork, honesty, and energy, each one described in a paragraph. Then we handed it over to employee focus groups. They were thoughtful, but liberal with their criticism. "This sounds like what every company promises," one said. To a reference about "drinking our own Kool-Aid," one response was "Kill it." The section on energy drew this criticism: "First sentence sounds weird—like we've hooked all our employees up to a wheel and are spinning."

So we kept at it, and the document got shorter, more precise, and closer to our vision. Each value could be expressed in a single sentence. And eventually, one of our stars, Drew Fortin, arranged the values in an acronym that everyone could remember and refer to: **THREADS**.

Teamwork: Focus on the We, not the Me.

Honesty: Follow your moral compass.

Reliability: Be someone others can count on.

Energy: Be balanced. Be energized.

Action: Errors of action are better than errors of inaction. Be brave.

Drive: Own it.

Scope: Don't try to boil the ocean.

The point I'm making here isn't that we're so fantastic, much less that readers should cut and paste these values. What's meaningful is that it caught on. Today, people actually use the word "threads" as a shorthand for the way things should work at the company. Employees have even launched a THREADS channel on Slack, where folks give their colleagues public kudos for demonstrating one or more of the values.

We're now creating another set of values, **FABRIC**, for our leadership channel. It guides employees through the goals and priorities of advancing as managers. They include:

Followership and vision: Be someone others want to follow.

Awareness of oneself: Lead with humility and grace.

Business skills: Understand the big picture.

Results and accountability: Set the bar at great.

Instruction and mentorship: Place a high value on helping others.

Courage: Stretch beyond your comfort zone for the greater good.

The lesson I learned through this process is that the culture you want doesn't simply evolve. You have to work at it, define it, evangelize it, live it, and share it every day. Culture is intentional.

NEXT STEPS

○ If you haven't defined your culture, bring together your top team and most important employees and do it. It must be real. (If it has even a trace of BS, it will be worthless.)

○ Monitor tools like Glassdoor, kununu, and Blind to see if your culture comes through in reviews of and comments about your company. If there's a gap, address it.

○ Customize questions in your 360 review process around your culture.

Building Dream Teams

On a spring day in 2017, a 25-year-old English sailor and boatbuilder named Leo Goolden climbed down into the bowels of a wreck of a sailing ship called *Tally Ho*. The wood was rotting, the century-old planks of teak and oak turning into mulch. *Tally Ho*, which hadn't been seaworthy for decades, was headed for the scrapyard.

Goolden admired the bones of the boat; she had a pedigree and a storied career. He had seen a photo of *Tally Ho* in her triumphant prime, in full sail, winning the storied Fastnet Race in 1927. What would it take, he wondered, to rescue her and return the old ship to her glory?

With that, Goolden embarked on an ambitious renovation project. Some might call it insanity. He bought the wreck for a symbolic British pound and cajoled a friend in the coastal village of Sequim, Washington, to let Goolden convert his back lawn into an improvised shipyard.

Practically the entire ship would have to be taken apart and remade anew. Goolden knew it would have been far easier and cheaper simply to build a new one. But, as Goolden later explained to members of the Royal Ocean and Racing Club in London, "There is just something about an old boat, and keeping the history alive. It's such a romantic and inspiring idea, and that made me want to do it, I suppose."

He couldn't do it alone. He would need help and, of course, money. So he would have to evangelize and infect others with this romantic and inspiring vision. To this end, he created a series of neatly produced and edited videos, each one an engaging first-person journal entry of the latest task at hand, whether it was installing transom timbers or sanding, chamfering, and varnishing the deck beams. No matter how grueling the task, he made it look like a good time. The friendly animals he kept around, including a parrot named Pancho, added warmth and humor, much as they do in Disney productions.

Goolden posted the videos on YouTube, and they caught on. Pretty soon he had hundreds of people sending him money every month. A Facebook group dedicated to *Tally Ho* gained more than 5,000 followers. But most important, for the purposes of this chapter: people with valuable skills began knocking at his door in Sequim. They wanted to pitch in.

Leo Goolden, through the allure of his message and the passion of his quest, was putting together a dream team.

Very few of us are engaged in projects as romantic as resuscitating a sailing ship. Building air conditioners, selling life insurance, or microtargeting banner ads cannot conjure up the same magic. And most of us, no matter how hard we try, won't succeed in building global audiences around our day-to-day business on YouTube.

And yet, Goolden's *Tally Ho* endeavor holds lessons for us. At the beginning of each of his videos, he says, "Hi," looking at the camera with his lopsided smile. "My name's Leo. I'm a boatbuilder and a sailor, and"—then he mentions the key word—"I'm on a *mission* to rebuild and restore . . ."

It is the sense of mission that grabs people's attention. It promises a narrative, a journey from here to there, the kind of story we've followed addictively since our Cro-Magnon days. In companies, a clear sense of mission provides a team not just with a goal, but also a purpose.

Business executives have known this for a long time, and over recent decades they have crafted mission statements. Once a company reaches a certain size, this exercise is often viewed as obligatory—and it often feels like it. Some board subcommittee throws together a few clichés, and it's featured prominently in the annual report and on the orientation materials for new hires. More often than not, these statements end up in the recycling bin. But in my explorations, I've found mission statements that come close to Leo Goolden's, which offer people a compelling journey, a destination, a purpose. They entice people not just to experience the story, but to lend their time and talent to it.

For some companies, this is easier than for others. Elon Musk's SpaceX, for example, is basically *Tally Ho* on steroids, one looking to the future instead of the past. Here's how Musk sells it:

> You want to wake up in the morning and think the future is going to be great—and that's what being a spacefaring civilization is all about. It's about believing in the future and thinking that the future will be better than the past. And I can't think of anything more exciting than going out there and being among the stars.

While Musk evokes the excitement of extending human life beyond earth, the Bill and Melinda Gates Foundation focuses on people's dreams to save billions of fellow earth-lings. It's a big and bold endeavor.

> We seek to unlock the possibility inside every individual. We see equal value in all lives. And so we are dedicated to improving the quality of life for individuals around the world. From the education of students in Chicago, to the health of a young mother in Nigeria, we are catalysts of human promise everywhere.

Google's original mission statement, when it debuted as a search engine, was simpler, but also compelling:

> Our company mission is to organize the world's information and make it universally accessible and useful.

At The Predictive Index, we appeal to people's desire to figure out how the human condition manifests at work. Our software and services use this information to guide you in building great companies with extremely happy and productive teams.

> Our passion, inherited from our founder, is to understand workplace behavior—specifically how people think and get work done. Our quest, like yours, is to learn how to play into their strengths, ignite their enthusiasm, and match them to the best jobs and teams. A good match creates a surplus of energy that positively impacts their work product, their team members, their families, and the greater world around them. We are creating better work and a better world.

While many executives view the company mission statement as an irksome homework assignment, in truth, it provides a foundational opportunity for attracting talent and focusing it on a goal. A common objective fuels engagement. It's the first step toward building perfect teams.

WHAT GAME ARE YOU PLAYING?

Whether the team you're building is the Oakland A's or the night shift at General Motors, the first questions are simple: What game are you playing, and in what league? The answers will help determine what type of employees you'll need, how much you'll have to pay them, and what kind of training you'll have to provide.

What are the psychometric qualities needed? As we've discussed, the actuarial department of an insurance company might build its team with lots of meticulous detail people, while a shock-jock radio program would shop for extroverts. How important is the cognitive piece? Smarts tend to cost a lot. But for some jobs social skills or patience might be more valuable.

Looking around at competitors is, of course, vital. They set the status quo for skills and pay for the league you're in.

Sometimes a shift in strategy changes the picture. When my business partner and I bought our first company, LEDCO, the company was marketing its equipment—technology housing for police cars, what we called "rugged peripherals"—by appealing directly to the cops. The salespeople were motorheads. They had a big black Crown Victoria that was tricked out with all their gear, all the radios and monitors. It looked like an undercover police car. They'd pull up to the back door of police stations carrying coffee and a box of doughnuts in an effort to build a relationship with the mechanics that serviced the vehicles, who they hoped would proceed to bug their bosses for the upgrades.

That business model leaned heavily on people who could connect with those on the mechanical side. In the PI scheme, the lower-left quadrant, Process & Precision, was that sweet spot.

By the time we bought the company in 2004, the technology was shifting. Radio was on its way out, and the computer was on the rise, with the smartphone close behind. The business, like so many others, was pivoting toward information technology. Our sales approach shifted, as did our needs for talent. Instead of informal doughnuts with mechanics, we set up formal meetings with their bosses, with our sales teams walking through the front door at the appointed time, prepared to deliver polished PowerPoint demonstrations.

These were not mechanical sales, but presentations focused on value. Our sales teams stressed comfort, safety, quality, and above all, productivity. They had to own the room and discuss software compatibility, uptime, and the financial benefits of reliable systems. The talent for these jobs required less credibility about turning a wrench and more on the value of keeping a car on the road. In today's world, if any of multiple computers are down, the car is virtually useless. This shifted our needs to the lower-right corner, the Results & Discipline quadrant.

We knew what kind of people we needed, but there was also a quality factor. We wanted the top 10 percent. In a purely statistical sense, it would seem as though we'd have to pay top dollar. As the saying goes, you get what you pay for. But that's not entirely true. People will sacrifice a few extra dollars they might get elsewhere for a promising work experience. This is a form of compensation arbitrage. I call it "bending the curve."

I'm not saying that we can be cheap (and certainly not in our high-priced Boston market). Our approach is to pay well enough so that money is not an issue, offering about the seventy-fifth percentile of the industry average. That makes us competitive and takes compensation questions off the table. But we lean heavily on culture and vision to bend the curve, attracting top 10-percent candidates for top 25-percent compensation. We pull this off by convincing them that they'll do great and purposeful work, and also have fun.

This is arbitrage—zeroing in on the spread between cost and value. I should note that the benefits of this arbitrage don't last too long. Efficient markets tend to whittle down the gaps. Big stars eventually add so much value that they claim their top market value, either by getting raises or jumping to a competitor. So while paying at the seventy-fifth percentile often doesn't last long in our company, it's a useful benchmark for hiring.

Sometimes it's not an easy sell. In our early days at LEDCO, this was a special challenge. The office we moved into had an infestation of flying bugs. The paint was flaking off the walls. And yet we had to convince top candidates that we held keys to a bright future. One time, I was interviewing a 27-year-old wunderkind engineer and salesperson, Nic Milani. He had worked at Motorola and was a dream prospect for our company. But why would he ever choose our shop over a name-brand suitor? This was a major curve-bending exercise.

The bugs were flying around as we talked. You could hear the roar of trains passing on the tracks just out back. Humor helped. But what brought him in was the vision we spun. We were building something special and fun. We were putting together a dream team, and he was going to be a key player. It worked, and he played a big role.

This happens in professional sports all the time. Many of the players are already rich but still hungry for the ultimate goal in their career: a championship. That's the mission. In the 2008 Olympics, superstars LeBron James, Dwyane Wade, and Chris Bosh played on the US gold-medal team. They liked each other. So the three figured out a way to pursue their mission, creating an NBA dream team of their own in Miami. Each one settled for a bit less than market pay so that there would be enough to hire teammates, and many of those teammates also came in at steeply discounted pay. The shining mission they shared bent the curve mightily. Over the following four years, their team, the Miami Heat, went to the finals every year and won two NBA championships.

Not every workplace can offer championships and adulation, and some pale in comparison to competitors. Let's say you're in the software industry, and your company has carved out a niche in middleware. It's vital code, but no one ever sees it. The college classmate of one of your coders has landed at a virtual reality startup. They're working on Half Life: Alyx and Defector, two of the hottest games, and are on the verge of recruiting one of your stars. How can a middleware company compete with that?

Here it might make sense to focus on growth opportunities. This is a huge issue for ambitious employees, and according to a 2020 study by Oxford Economics, only 51 percent of employees say that their company offers them a chance to grow.* In this hypothetical case, you might discuss what sticking with you could mean down the road. Perhaps you're planning an international expansion. Would the star programmer be interested in moving to Guangzhou or Berlin, or even running one of those units? Discussing your plans and his hope might enable you to find a common path. If this is a vision you believe in, it shouldn't be that hard to evangelize.

METRICS FOR A DREAM TEAM

Let's assume you have a clear mission and a message. You have a team, and seems to be clicking. What metrics can you put to use to hone that group into a dream team?

Engagement, which we discussed in the last chapter, is a key metric. After testing, you can map the level of engagement across the company, placing the most engaged employees

---

* https://www.oxfordeconomics.com/workforce2020.

near the top, the disengaged toward the bottom. Each one of those dots has a name. This is essential data.

But it's even more useful if you combine engagement with performance. At our company, we chart the workforce into quadrants, placing everyone into a now familiar 2x2 format (Figure 6.1).

FIGURE 6.1 Engagement by Performance

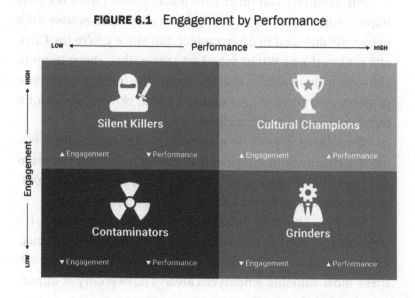

Under ideal conditions, you'll have lots of employees in the upper-right quadrant. Those people are worth gold. They're your Cultural Champions. You'd think that these would be the easiest people to manage, and in many ways they are. They're self-starters, and they tend to operate at a high time strata, which means they don't need much day-to-day guidance. They put in loads of discretionary effort.

However, you should still pay a lot of attention to them because it's around them that the company's culture and performance revolves. They deserve opportunities for leadership and assignments that will give them a chance to shine. So pay attention to their engagement surveys. Are they happy with their manager? If not, fix it. Some 80 percent of the people who leave a company do it to escape a manager. Also, sit down with them and learn what they like about their jobs and the company. Then—and this is crucial—make sure you don't take it away.

For example, you meet with a star coder. (She's not that happy, truth be told, to be sitting down with you, because she's extremely engaged in a key project. But since you're the CEO, she makes time.) When asked what she likes about her job, she says, a bit pointedly, that she enjoys the freedom to pursue projects at her own (high) speed, without slowing down for a bunch of meetings and reviews.

The following week, at a meeting, you're discussing a few underperformers. A few people in the tech department seem a bit lost. A colleague suggests dedicating two half-hour sessions a week to review results and keep everyone aligned.

Maybe . . . but *only* if you can give that star coder a pass. It's important, of course, to take steps to lift the laggards. But their needs should not make the stars unhappy or bored. After all, these most valuable employees always have plenty of opportunities elsewhere.

Nurturing the top performers in that upper-right quadrant is important not only for production, but also their contribution to the culture. If they're engaged and happy at work, that spirit can spread to others.

An analysis on a vast set of data made it clear early this century that happiness is contagious. In the study, Nicholas Christakis, a professor of medical sociology at Harvard Medical School, and James Fowler, a University of California political scientist, analyzed data from 4,700 children of volunteers from the massive 1948 Framingham Heart Study. Using a simple questionnaire, they followed the trails and linkages of happiness. They found that happy people tended to have more connections with other happy people. "Each additional happy person makes you happier," Christakis later said.*

This, of course, includes happiness at work. How could it not? Work is central to our lives and, in ideal cases, a source of achievement, community, and pride. Being happy at work goes hand in hand with being a happy parent, spouse, and friend; in short, with leading the kind of life that every human being would choose: being content.

A similar contagion, sadly, can spread in the opposite direction. For that, let's shift our focus to the most problematic quadrant, the lower left. The people there not only underperform, they are also disengaged. This is a toxic combination. We call these people, with all due respect, Contaminators. If cheerful productivity emanates from the upper-right quadrant, the Contaminators emit workplace poison. Their negative spirit, if allowed to fester, can spread to all four quadrants.

I want to make it clear that despite the colorful name we give them, these Contaminators are not to blame for the problem, and they're not bad people. Their troubles might represent a failure of management. Perhaps there's a fix. Maybe, though, they're not well suited for the job, or the company, and would be much happier and more successful elsewhere. In any case, even in the best-run companies, Contaminators represent 10 to 15 percent of the workforce. Dealing with this lower quartile is a job that never goes away, but one that must be done. Contaminators represent a clear and present danger to your team.

If you're engaged in a corporate turnaround or a change in strategy, you can assume that about 20 percent of the workforce will embrace it eagerly. Many of those will be in the upper-right quadrant, the Cultural Champions. The middle

---

* https://www.reuters.com/article/us-happiness/happiness-is-contagious-study-idUSTRE4B400H20081205.

60 percent will need to be convinced. And the remaining 20 percent will dig in their heels and resist. A good number of these recalcitrant employees, you can bet, will be in the Contaminator quadrant.

Let's say you carry out the engagement survey, blend that data with performance, and see your team for the first time on the 2x2 chart. Imagine your team has 100 employees, which means 100 dots, with 10 of them in the lower-left quadrant. That's not a terrible rate. But still, what to do with those 10 underperforming, not entirely zeroed-in colleagues?

Every now and then, there's an adjustment that works. One underperformer in marketing, when discussing her job, mentions that she majored in graphic design but fell into marketing because there were jobs there. But the analysis is heavily focused on statistics, which aren't her thing. Maybe this person could be a star in the design department.

Such fixes, unfortunately, are unusual. In most cases, lifting up the Contaminators is a bear. It requires engaging them, pushing them not only to do better at their job, but to focus on it. The process might include some training or learning a new skill.

It's a grind and the payoff, in truth, is uncomfortably low. Each struggling person represents nothing less than a turnaround project. My dictum is that in a small to midsized company, management doesn't have the bandwidth for more than one of these reclamations. Generally speaking, investments in other quartiles provide better returns.

This brings us to the subject of Happy Alumni. These are employees who leave the company, but with warm feelings and, hopefully, lasting friendships and connections. The idea is that the company and the employee tried something, and it didn't turn out so well. So now the company helps the employee land a better opportunity elsewhere. The executive team plies contacts at other companies. The colleague leaves with no shame and an industry-plus severance package. When Happy Alumni leave our company, we tell them that we might reunite, either at this company or another one in which we're involved. The relationship continues.

This may seem like a high-minded approach, and it might sound like I'm bragging. But the great thing is that caring for people this way brings all kinds of trickle-down benefits. With every good word they spread about you, for example, your hiring brand improves. Your ratings on Glassdoor inch up. That means you can hire more people who, hopefully, perform in the vaunted upper-right quadrant.

The changing chart says it all. If nine Happy Alumni depart, that quadrant empties out for the moment, and more dots pop up on the productive right side. This move to the right side of the chart is perpetual for successful companies. It's essential for optimizing talent.

I should add that not all of the Happy Alumni are poor performers. Sometimes people who do excellent work want to leave. They get an offer for a lot more money. They want to move with their partner to Santa Fe. They've decided to write screenplays. Whatever the reason, they're leaving. They, too, can be—must be—Happy Alumni. They leave, spread the word about the company, and a good number of them find their way back.

SILENT KILLERS

Looking at the quadrant above the Contaminators, you'll find a group of workers who are much more engaged in their jobs. However, their results, sadly, are subpar. These are known as the Silent Killers.

You wouldn't know they're a problem from looking at them. Unlike their daydreaming Contaminator colleagues, the Silent Killers are fully wrapped up in the company. They like it here! They chat with teammates in the coffee space, pop into cubicles and lament last night's Red Sox debacle. Some of them take the company's mission seriously and offer interesting insights at meetings. They're committed, in their way. Trouble is, they just don't do the greatest work.

Again, it's not easy. Becoming a better worker isn't guaranteed. Those people need to buy into a transformation. If they don't own the problem, they won't own the solution.

The turnaround requires a lot of hands-on attention, starting with regular meetings to match targets to results. Keep the time frame short to give the turnaround a sense of urgency, and consider hooking them up with strong mentors in the company. Sometimes this rigorous effort pays off, and those successes feel magical. A subpar performer develops into a star.

This is exhilarating, in part, because it's not common. Only a minority of Silent Killers makes it to the productive right side of the chart. Old habits die hard.

The better payoff resides in the opposite, lower-right quadrant, the realm of the Grinders. These are people who do fantastic work and then seem to disappear at least mentally for a few days or weeks. The quality of their efforts, when they're engaged, is top rate. Trouble is, their minds *at* work aren't entirely focused *on* work.

The Grinder quadrant is where the greatest potential lies. Unlike colleagues in the two low-performing quadrants to the left, the Grinders are capable of excellence. A lot of people, despite training and years of effort, never achieve the star level of the Grinder. When the Grinder is engaged, that person may be every bit as productive or brilliant as the treasured Cultural Champions. Trouble is that the Grinders are not fully engaged.

Engage them, and you have new stars. Don't wait another day.

The key is to get to the root of the engagement problem. It's important to make it clear to them from the get-go that they are valued, and that if they have troubles or frustrations, the company is ready to help in any way it can. It might mean adjusting their schedule to fit with custody arrangements, or switching managers who provide more guidance, or perhaps less. Whatever the case, get feedback and take action. These are valuable workers, and they are worth substantial investments in time and money.

THE 2x2 HACK

Let's say you'd like to plot your team members in the four quadrants of the 2x2 chart, but you have no tools on hand to measure performance and engagement. Don't despair. You can get started with an easy hack.

It's based on "forced ranking." This is a method of ranking the employees by comparing them to each other, not to a fixed metric. Bob outperforms Sam. Caroline tops Bob. Pretty soon you have a ranking. This method has all kinds of vulnerabilities. It certainly embeds biases. But it's a quick way to generate data for a 2x2 chart.

Do forced ranking for both performance and engagement, giving each employee a numerical ranking for each. Then plot them on the chart.

This is an imprecise measurement, and it might not be fair. However, it serves to focus attention. Outside of the upper-right quadrant, whose inhabitants are deemed both engaged and high performing, everyone else on the chart appears to be lacking—at least relatively—in either performance or engagement, or both.

Performance can often be addressed en masse. Low performers must go (maybe leave room for one reclamation project). The fix is in establishing a threshold.

Addressing engagement, I find, is more like weeding. Each case must be dealt with individually. It requires digging and connecting.

As I've said, you'll get the biggest bang for your buck by zeroing in on the Grinders, the people in the lower-right quadrant. They do great work when they're into it. The challenge is to get them engaged.

How to do that? Figuring out the source of disengagement requires investigation. My advice is for the manager to have a periodic meeting with each direct report, with a special focus on Grinders. These sit-downs should have a different feel from a team meeting because the talk is going to be about bigger issues, such as life and happiness.

I find that going out for a beer often works well, but it could be lunch or a coffee. Open up about some of your own work-life issues, and ask them about theirs: kids, health, diet, career goals. Are they under stress? Are there aspects of the job they don't like? Could they use a vacation?

If you haven't established a culture of openness, this conversation won't go too far, at least the first time around. It's still worth doing, though, as a step toward building trust. The key is to give them a clear sense that you're there to help.

And who knows, the reason for the disengagement might be a simple preference. One project excites her, she tells you, and this other one bores her to tears. Turning this Grinder into a star may simply be a matter of giving her a larger helping of the work she likes.

The key for building dream teams, after all, is expanding the population of the upper-right quadrant, the Cultural Champions. The Grinders have what it takes. It's just a matter of engaging them.

NEXT STEPS

- Meet with your team to analyze your mission statement. How compelling is it? Is it accessible? Memorable? Does it align your people? Does it help your hiring brand? If not, redo it.
- Discuss tools you use to measure performance and engagement. If you have none, acquire them and start measuring.
- Plot your workforce on the 2x2 chart, starting with managers. Then have them do it with their teams. Use the charts for discussions on which employees to invest in and which to convert into Happy Alumni.

Coaching

From the days of the ancient Phoenicians through much of the twentieth century, the sea captain had a singular job. He—and it was always a he—fit a certain profile. Whether transporting Vikings, conquistadors, or crossing the Pacific with a cargo of rubber duckies from China, the captain had to be a strong, unquestioned leader, who was decisive and a keen judge of risk. After all, each voyage posed dangers: typhoons, pirates, even threats of mutiny. The fate of the ship rested on the captain's judgment and character.

By the 1990s, though, the job was changing, and executives at the biggest shipping company in the world, Maersk, took notice. With global positioning satellites and better weather modeling, "quants" in offices could track and route the ships, which were now transporting nearly everything in standardized containers. From offices in Copenhagen, they could guide legions of ships along the safest and most efficient routes.

With these changes, Maersk no longer needed imperious leaders captaining their ships (and frankly, questioning their orders). What they required instead was a well-organized type who attended to details and followed orders. How would they find the people to meet this profile?

Their search led them to personality assessment. They began testing the captains and new recruits alike for a host of traits, including dominance, communication styles, patience, and need for structure.

In the old days, Maersk hired captains who appeared to be sky-high in dominance, with the requisite sensitivity for risk. But now they were in the market for an altogether different breed of captain. The model was not Sir Francis Drake or Admiral Halsey, but instead a helpful concierge at a Hilton.

Within a few years, Maersk saw that the test worked not just for captains, but for every job in the company. Certain personalities were ideal for deckhands, others for engineers. Maersk began to optimize its entire workforce.

It was during this time that Jixuan Wang, a Chinese executive for the shipping company, mastered the Maersk approach. It opened his eyes to a business opportunity. He knew that there was a near limitless supply of unskilled labor in the poor interior of China. Some of the more ambitious young people emigrated toward the coast, to booming cities like Shanghai and Guangzhou. But far more, many of them both capable and intelligent, stayed behind. With the proper training, they could become highly productive merchant marines who might outperform the incumbents—dominated by Filipinos—and perhaps at lower cost.

In 2002, Wang started Sinocrew, a service to groom and provide crews for ships worldwide. He leaned heavily on cognitive and psychometric assessments to sniff out the most promising prospects. His recruiters toured the towns and cities of the Chinese interior offering a free educational opportunity that could lead to an international career. Lots of people were interested. They took the assessments, and Sinocrew had its pick of the candidates. They chose those with cognitive skills above a certain threshold, and then consulted the psychometric charts to assign each to a job track that made the most sense: Cultivators toward customer service, for example, or Process-dominant types toward engine maintenance. They created a career development plan for each one, and forged them into seafarers at the Shanghai academy.

The schooling took two years. Financial returns would be slow in coming, but Wang had patient investors. For them, it was an arbitrage opportunity. There was an enormous gap between the cost of untrained field workers and the value that they would produce once they emerged from the academy.

What Wang set up in Shanghai was a mini Naval Academy, with stunning parallels to the one I attended for one year in Annapolis. What I saw in Shanghai was like a flashback. At Annapolis, Plebes, as freshmen are known, had to run up and down the stairs, always on the outside, so as not to intrude on our more leisurely superiors—the upperclassmen—who were permitted a slower pace. We had to be close enough to the wall to click it with our heels.

Sure enough, in Shanghai, the Chinese Plebes were scampering up and down the stairs, doing everything but clicking the walls. Far beyond these rituals, they were learning the discipline and skills of seamen. When I visited, 1,000 students were enrolled, equaling about 25 percent of the student body at Annapolis. Now Sinocrew, with its base in Beijing and operations in multiple Chinese cities, has 10,000 of its graduates deployed on ships around the world.

THE HUMANITY IN TALENT OPTIMIZATION

Sometimes when I describe my passion for talent optimization, I see people shrink back. I can tell what they're thinking before they even open their mouths. They look at the assessments and the charts as tools to automate the management of labor and to strip away humanity. They see algorithms running through the data and dropping people into buckets, much the way Facebook targets us for advertisements and Amazon optimizes us as shoppers. In short, they see our company as a close relative of Sinocrew's academy in Shanghai.

What I'm helping to build (and I hope it's clear by now) is by no means automated. Effective talent optimization involves bringing humans far more in touch with each other—communicating more with greater honesty, listening, and seeking out feedback. The tools simply provide more insights. I imagine that this is true even at Sinocrew's academy. No one is better at understanding or motivating each of us than a fellow human being.

I do not hold up Sinocrew as a model of cutting-edge talent optimization—its training model is copied from age-old practices at the Naval Academy—but Sinocrew is a vital showcase for the fundamental value of coaching. A culture of coaching adds three essentials:

1. It creates a system of accountability, both up and down.
2. It develops expertise because coaches have been there before.
3. It adds perspective. Coaches have a broader vision of the company and industry terrain that an employee is navigating. They can spot both the dangers and the opportunities.

You can see this dynamic, in all of its dimensions, at the gym. Picture the scene. People are riding exercise bikes and lifting weights. Most are listening to music or podcasts, or even talking on the phone. While a few seem to be getting pretty good workouts, others are taking it easy, putting in time.

Then there's a woman over at the bench press who has a personal trainer. He's watching her, making sure that she's pushing straight up and not at an angle. Under his guidance, she's working harder and smarter than everyone else. It might be raining outside or horribly cold, but she doesn't blow off this Tuesday night session. She's accountable to her coach, as he is to her. For that same reason, she pushes herself harder than the people who aren't being monitored. When she feels a pain in her shoulder, she can ask the coach about it. He's got expertise. And he has the perspective to tell her how hard she'll have to work, and how long, to get the results she wants. There's a reason people swear by personal trainers, if they can afford them. They get results.

In business, coaching adds essential value. In the crudest math, it raises the performance of the company's most important asset, whether by 10 percent, 100 percent, or 300 percent. Even more important, good coaching lifts people's engagement, and it can lead to value that cannot even be measured, building teamwork, increasing happiness, and spawning groundbreaking ideas. Success hinges on harvesting the value gap between what a player is and what he or she can be. I like to think of it, as financiers do, as arbitrage.

Conversely, an employee's coachability is a marker for success—and failure. According to a survey by Leadership IQ, a research firm, the leading cause for employee failure is a resistance to coaching (Figure 7.1).

In sports, some coaches develop rigid systems. Year in and year out, they take players through the same drills, reaching for the same benchmarks, even shouting out the same blend of curses and encouragement. Those with a good and well-executed system can be consistently successful.

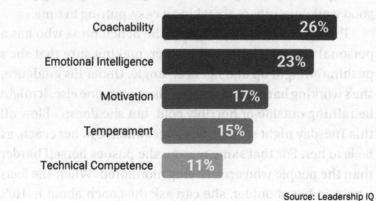

FIGURE 7.1 Leading deficits causing employee failure

Coachability	26%
Emotional Intelligence	23%
Motivation	17%
Temperament	15%
Technical Competence	11%

Source: Leadership IQ

But the goal here is not to settle for being a dedicated coach, or even a good one. The objective is to be great. And the greatest ones do not repeat a winning formula year in, year out. They adjust to the individuals they are coaching. They figure them out, using whatever tools and metrics they have, including their own people skills, and then adjust the coaching to what will click with each player.

This is what Pat Summitt mastered, as I described in the Introduction. She knew the psychometrics of each player on her championship teams. When she traveled to the rural town of Sparta, Tennessee, to recruit a tough-minded, 5-foot-10 guard named Kellie Jolly, she knew enough about Jolly to develop an individual development plan. The guard was a perfectionist who demanded clear goals and the metrics to measure her progress. Summit knew how to provide this. The coach also had enough perspective to foresee what Jolly, with great coaching, could become: the point guard for a championship team. (Jolly went onto a coaching career of her own, and in the spring of 2019, she was hired to take on Pat Summitt's old job as head coach of the Lady Vols.)

This customized approach not only draws more from each person but also widens the pool of available talent. Often in business, as in sports, certain talented people don't fit. It might be a successful system, whether at McKinsey and Company or the Boston Celtics, but certain people just don't work out. They become unhappy. Production dips. They are deemed difficult, or malcontents. In the talent marketplace, their value plummets.

For a great coach, these misfits represent mouthwatering arbitrage opportunities. They're undervalued and brimming with potential. Some could be stars. In a sense, they're similar to the Grinders I mentioned in the previous chapter—those employees who do excellent work but aren't fully engaged. The coaching challenge, whether for Grinders or those deemed "difficult," is to figure out what they need to be successful, and how best to integrate them into a team.

I encountered this when I was coaching the US Olympic sailing team for the 1996 Atlanta games. There was a supremely talented sailor named Kristina Farrar. According to the Myers-Briggs Type Indicator, which was the assessment tool I knew back then, she was a strong S. That stands for "Sensing." These super-analytical people demand the facts, not a bunch of ideas wrapped up in anecdotes. They trust experience much more than words or symbols. They like data. They're not big on analogies.

Farrar worked with a legendary coach, Skip Whyte, whose teams had won numerous world and national championships. Whyte had a fabulous technical eye. He spied on every boat, and figured out why they were fast. He tended to communicate in stories. This worked brilliantly for many of his athletes. He was a great coach—for them. But his style drove Kristina Farrar nuts. She wanted clear information, and instead got analogies she had to decipher. She was a highly talented sailor who was unhappy. "Never let Skip Whyte talk to me again," she told me. "All he does is piss me off." In some systems, she might have been deemed a malcontent. But all she needed was an informational fix.

So I took it upon myself to interpret Skip Whyte, putting his coaching into a framework that worked for her. (This didn't come naturally to me because I, too, am a nonlinear thinker. According to Myers-Briggs, I am an N, for Intuition.) She became happier and melded well with the team. (You might not be surprised to learn that after her Olympic career, Kristina Farrar followed her analytical skills to become a quant at a top financial firm.)

NEARLY EVERYONE IS A COACH

Think about your company. Who are the coaches? In some places, they work in a development or training wing run by Human Resources. Other companies outsource the job to consultants. Lots of businesses barely bother with it at all.

But for talent optimization, everyone who manages, even if it's only one or two people, has to be a coach. This should be central to the job. Your success, after all, hinges on the performance of the people reporting to you, your team, whether you're a CEO or a sales manager. And the way to lift their performance is to coach them.

How to start? The assessments are helpful. But the most important step is simply to have a conversation. When I take a coaching approach with my employees, I ask them to tell me about their careers and where, in the very best of cases, they see themselves in five years.

My job, I tell them, is to help them get there and achieve their goals. Together we will map out a pathway in that direction. These career discussions are central to the relationship, and should guide it from the start. It's key to helping them along their path, whether it leads them up the company ranks or elsewhere. Throughout this process, each employee requires constant oversight, feedback, and, above all, coaching.

For them to listen to me, and be frank and open, they have to know that I have their backs—that my goal is to assist them, and that I will not use the information they share with me to do anything but support them.

I work to gain this trust from the beginning. One good way, I've found, is to tell them about my struggles, my weaknesses: all the baggage on the back of my T-shirt. Making yourself vulnerable to gain trust is basic animal behavior. Dogs do it by rolling over and exposing their bellies.

In these talks I explain that our objective is to build a corporate culture that revolves around people. It accepts a few basic premises: Each one of us is a work in progress. We are all striving to reach our goals, as individuals and teams. To this end, we help each other. The foundation for this is constant and caring coaching, built upon honest communication, the bad as well as the good.

If an employee knows that you care about her and her career and that you want her to succeed, she doesn't mind nearly as much when you tell her exactly how she might have handled something better. It's still no fun. But she knows that you're trying to help, that you're not tearing her down. You can read all of the unwelcome items from the back of her T-shirt and even help her add to the list, but you still have her back.

Strong support and honest communication also keep strong performers onboard. According to PI data, 94 percent of employees with good or great bosses say they have passion and energy for their jobs. Then there are the 41 percent of respondents unhappy with their managers, who report little passion and energy for their work. So they leave. Some 77 percent of people working for bad bosses say they want out within a year.

Each of us will have different strengths as coaches and varying approaches, depending on our personalities. Some coaches move faster with more structure, while others stress the personal relationships.

We have one coach in our sales department, Jim Speredelozzi, who has organized level after level of coaching within a highly disciplined training and development program. It's process driven with a laser focus on results.

The way he sees it, his job is to build a training machine. He prefers novice salespeople because they don't assume that they already know the job. Each one is a clean slate. On day one, they begin a four-step process with an eye to graduating, two years later, as a bona fide sales star. As people advance to the second, third, and fourth levels, they coach the people coming up behind them. So each person in the second stage works with colleagues in the first and holds them accountable for reaching targets.

I sat in on a session not long ago. A team was listening to a new associate on a sales call. I took notes for 10 minutes, thinking that I'd be able to give great feedback from the very top. But giving feedback is one of the skills they work on. And when the call was finished, they asked a young associate to weigh in. He'd been with the program for only eight months.

I figured he would deliver a few insights before handing it over to me. Then I would advance the process immeasurably. In the end, as you might have guessed, he provided high-quality and insightful feedback, with a caring touch. It was better than I could have done, so I kept my mouth shut.

By the end of this two-year program, employees have job skills that make them more valuable, wherever they go. But the immediate payoff is for the company. Reducing it purely to financial arbitrage, Jim gets the performance of a $150,000 per year star from a relative newcomer who makes barely half as much.

Establishing clear career paths within an organization certainly takes time and effort. But in the end, I'd argue, it provides both employees and their coaches with vital guidance. And it often saves time. After all, people constantly want to know about the criteria for moving up, what gets measured, and how and where they can climb. They should know from the get-go, and their coach should be on top of it too.

THE BELICHICK MODEL

If you look at the four dimensions of the PI behavioral chart, it's probably not difficult to figure out where you stand. For many, in fact, the assessment largely confirms and codifies what they already know. That's why it can seem magical. You look at it and say, "That's me!"

So let's assume that you start out coaching *without* the tools. There are still ways to extract a lot of the benefits simply by analyzing people, including yourself. This amounts to hacking personality optimization. It involves focusing on which qualities the coach and the team members would likely exhibit, and then anticipating their needs and preferences.

Take Bill Belichick (Figure 7.2), the irascible championship coach of the New England Patriots. He's won more Super Bowls than any coach in NFL history. Since fans have been watching him for decades, pacing up and down the sideline, clipboard in hand, wearing his trademark hoodie and a scowl, many of us feel we know him.

Even without an assessment, his personality is clear. He's high in dominance. He's direct, decisive, and supremely comfortable with conflict. He barks at players and referees. And if a reporter asks him a hard question after the game, Belichick simply glares at him, maybe uttering a monosyllable. He's confident in his ideas.

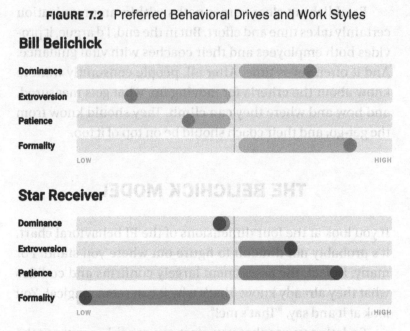

FIGURE 7.2　Preferred Behavioral Drives and Work Styles

Bill Belichick's behavioral drives were estimated by a panel of advanced PI practitioners based on observed behaviors and interviews.

At the same time, he's low on extroversion. No question about that. His communication style is supremely succinct.

Yet like many of us, Belichick appears to have a second dominant drive. He's extremely strong in Formality. He holds to a rigid structure. Rules are clear and beyond dispute. He insists that players attend meetings on time. And each player has specific assignments that are fundamental. They must fit into a system.

Belichick is data driven. He demands facts—not wishes, prayers, or opinions—and he goes to extraordinary lengths to get them. More than once, his team has been disciplined for training video cameras on the opponents' sideline, attempting to pick up coaching signals. Signals promise precious data, which Belichick could then incorporate into his scheme.

Self-knowledge, of course, is important. But the greater challenge for a coach is to understand the personality of each of the team members, and what type of coaching will bring out the best in them. A personality assessment tool like PI's has algorithms that produce relationship guides, telling each person what the other one needs and wants, and what will mostly likely drive them crazy.

But it's possible to hack a relationship guide. The starting point is a conversation. For Belichick, this involves sitting down with a player and learning what's going on in the rest of his life. "There are a lot of things that affect what happens on the field that occur off the field," he told an interviewer in 2017.* Players "have wives and girlfriends. And they have babies. And they have personal situations. They have parents that are sick. All of it runs in together."

In our personality hacking scenario, a great coach would focus not just on the player's personal situation, but also his personality. What are his dominant drives? Picture an immensely gifted wide receiver. He's extremely popular with his teammates, and is quick to provide support to them when they screw up. Yet there's something a bit carefree about him, even sloppy. He doesn't always run the routes as drawn up, because he likes to improvise, sometimes doing it brilliantly.

A coach with Belichick's behavioral drives would see that this carefee receiver is his polar opposite (refer to Star Receiver in Figure 7.2). The man is not a dominant personality, but instead a collaborator. And he doesn't stress on details— sometimes to the point of driving the coach crazy. This is not a match made in heaven. But a great coach understands that talent comes in many flavors. Without sacrificing his control over the team, the domineering coach could take steps to adapt to that player. This might mean putting him in group situations, and finding ways to give him freedom in certain areas. He might come up with the semblance of free choice in

---

* https://www.cnbc.com/2017/04/13/bill-belichick-leadership-rules.html.

a system that provides little of it. If his scheme, for example, gives equal chance of success to two different pass patterns, the coach might say, "You know, I think the inside curl works better here, but maybe the fly route. What do you think?"

But at the same time, the coach must also clearly establish the details, rules and routines that the receiver cannot ignore. The coach, after all, is the boss.

The key, whether running algorithmic relationship guides or hacking them, is for the coach to understand team members well enough to adjust, if only slightly, to their personalities. This involves a recognition that people have different styles, and they are much more likely to perform at their highest level if they get at least a recognition of their style from the coach.

The one advantage a coach like Belichick has over most of us in the corporate world is the allure of a championship ring. Players desperately want to win Super Bowls. The rings define their careers, and for many, their lives. Belichick's model clearly works and creates a winning culture. The upshot is that while he no doubt finds ways to bend to his players, they have an even stronger motivation to bend to him.

TSP: TRUTHFUL, SPECIFIC, POSITIVE

One key to coaching, which certainly is not foreign to Coach Belichick, is telling people when they do something wrong. But an effective coach should prepare the ground for such feedback. It involves telling them when they do something right. Michael Allosso—actor, director, and business consultant—provides wonderful guidance on this. The key, he says, is not just to tell people that they've done a good job. That's too easy, and too general. He calls for coaches to provide feedback that is truthful, specific, and positive, or TSP.

The key is the S. "I see Little League coaches say the same thing," he says. " 'You guys work really hard, and I love you all.' " The problem with such vague praise, Allosso says, is that no one knows if the coach has been paying attention. "If you add the specific, you tell someone exactly what impressed you. It's the specific that makes it rock. They glow." To come up with TSP, of course, it's essential to pay attention. In Allosso's words: "You've got to keep your eyes open and catch people doing things right."

And once the coaches have established that they see and appreciate the good, they have a more receptive audience when the time comes to point out shortcomings. "If you've given them the positive specific feedback," Allosso says, "it's as if you earn credits for the growth feedback. They're ready to listen, and know that you're there to help."

THE 360 REVIEW

In an ideal coaching scenario, communication is prolific and feedback is rampant. At the heart of our system is the annual 360 review. This provides each of us with a view of how others see us, both good and bad. It gives us a structure for addressing our shortcomings and enhancing our strengths. The value of the 360 increases over the years. By the time someone has been at the company for three or four years, the 360s map out their growth, their trends, and their recurring issues. It's a formidable tool.

For me, conducting 360s is central to my work as a coach. For each person who reports to me, I chose six to eight reviewers: a couple of them above the employee on the org chart, others at the same level, and a few below. It's important for each of us to understand how we're perceived at every level. I tell these reviewers to describe their colleague's strengths and shortcomings. These evaluations shouldn't take too long, no more than a half hour. The key is to get the important stuff on the table, and most of that comes out quickly.

There are all kinds of tools for running 360s. I detail a few of them in the Appendix. You can run a 360 on all kinds of technology, from notepads to Excel spreadsheets.

The anonymous reviews should cover both the front and back of the T-shirt: the employee's accomplishments on one side and what colleagues quietly gripe about on the other. For example, a star in sales might have numbers to die for, and be one of the highest paid people at the company. This is a high performer. Those impressive numbers grace the front of his T-shirt.

But the 360 might bring to the surface some other, less flattering details. Maybe he's conceited, and doesn't have time for others on his team. Maybe he mails it in for the first half of the month, and turbocharges it the last week to hit his targets. It's bad for morale, a couple of the reviewers say.

When I receive these six to eight reviews, I sit down with two colored pencils and a pen. I know this might sound a bit extreme, but there's a method. I want to highlight the Front of T-Shirt items in one color, and the Back of T-Shirt items with the other. I use the pen to take notes.

One of the things I look for is a high deviation among the reviewers. It points to a line of questioning. Why do certain people find more fault with you? Could it have to do with how you manage up or down? I also compare the employee's self-assessment with what others say. Are people being too hard on themselves? Do they seem to have blind spots?

Before I sit down with direct reports, I review their 360 from the previous year. What were the themes and the development plan? Have they made progress in those areas? I also pull up their psychometric charts and analyses. They may help explain some of the issues. Someone who's high in Dominance, for example, is more likely to steamroll colleagues, while another who's strong in Process might drive colleagues crazy with nitpicking. These behaviors won't change. But there are strategies to maximize the best qualities and to sand down the rough edges.

Once this preparation is done, it's time for the meeting. I usually schedule an hour and a half for each. I start by asking employees for their read of the assessments. Do they agree with them? Are there surprises?

When I jump in, it's with the positive. I go over their Front of T-Shirt accomplishments and numbers and try to reinforce the specific achievements of which they can be proud—Michael Allosso's TSP.

Early in these sessions, I usually bring up my own 360s and some of the Back of T-Shirt items with which I've been grappling. The idea is that all of us, even the CEO, have these issues and need to keep on top of them. By discussing my own challenges, I'm coaxing them to open up. Defensiveness in a 360 defeats its purpose.

At that point, we dip into the areas of weakness. Someone on the marketing team, for example, might be oversensitive to feedback. He takes criticism as an attack on his competence and becomes agitated, even combative. This makes it hard for others. It can shut down individual and group dynamics.

Simply identifying this as an issue is an important first step. The next is to identify triggers. Is it criticism from a certain person, whether superior or subordinate, that sets off this response? Is it when he perceives that they are not fully prepared or out of their range? Does he feel his pulse pick up or heat building in his face before one of these outbursts? Identifying the triggers is key to figuring out the workarounds. Dealing with this problem is an action item.

Maybe that same person did a bang-up job organizing a user conference. This is a big item on the front of his T-shirt.

How can he find other similar opportunities for his organizational gifts to shine? We nail down a couple. Two more action items. They go into the review.

In the following year's review, we see how he fared on those action items. As people go through year after year of 360s, they make progress. But they also can backslide. Take a team member who was over critical, a bit self-centered, and reluctant to celebrate wins with the team. Through hard work, he seemed to master these issues. But recently he's started to snap at colleagues, and complain that he's not getting enough credit. . . . Most of these Back of T-Shirt items are persistent. Keeping them at bay takes steady effort.

The 360 is an essential exercise for helping everyone be themselves on their best day. But the one thing that can screw up the entire dynamic is money. That is why coaching must be entirely divorced from even a whisper about compensation. The fear of losing a bonus or of making less money than teammates feeds anxiety and makes people think strategically. They keep secrets and hide stuff, which kills the 360.

Let's say a coder is in a big hurry to close a major project, and in his rush, he copies a few lines of code from another project that has not been vetted. He figures that it will function just as well, and it saves him a day of work, moving the project ahead. However, as luck would have it, the copied code includes a bug, unlicensed content, or worse, malware.

That's a big mistake. There's definitely going to be a difficult discussion, and it's essential that the coder provide every detail. It's not pleasant, but, hopefully, he knows that he is valued, that everyone makes mistakes, and that his coach is committed to helping him do his job better. All good.

But if the coaching is tied up with compensation, this painful communication is poisoned. He might fear that opening up about the extent of his mistake will cost him a chunk of his annual raise—if he gets one at all. That could be thousands of dollars. So perhaps he clams up. Or maybe he doesn't. But when he gets his raise, he wonders: Would it have been higher if I had kept my mouth shut?

Mixing coaching and compensation is toxic.

FOCUS ON STRENGTHS

In the 1990s, Pete Sampras was the best male tennis player on earth (at least the part of earth not covered with clay). But if you compared Sampras to other top stars, such as Andre Agassi, his ground strokes were a vulnerability. The longer the rally, the more likely Sampras was to lose the point.

Sampras's coach, Tim Gullikson, could have pushed him to focus on this one relative weakness and fix it. After all, Sampras had perhaps the strongest serve in the game. If he could lift his forehand and backhand to a similar level, he would be unstoppable. But Gullikson studied Sampras's statistics and noticed a significant correlation. When Sampras managed to get his first serve in more than 65 percent of the time, he always won.

Ten or 20 times in a match, Sampras's opponents couldn't even lay a racquet on his first serve. He aced them. And even when they managed to return it, the returns were often weak. On those points, Sampras would thunder toward the net and swat a winner. When his serve went in, he didn't need great ground strokes.

For Gullikson, the pathway to championships was clear. Instead of propping up Sampras's weak area, the key was to focus on his strength, adding consistency to his serve.

Gullikson, if we look at his coaching through our scheme, was focusing his attention on the front of the T-shirt. For more than a decade, Sampras was widely regarded as the best server in the world. It was on the front of his T-shirt. Of course, it wasn't exactly a secret to Sampras, or to anyone else, that his ground strokes weren't up to the standard of his nemesis, Agassi. TV commentators and tennis writers opined endlessly on the subject. The key for his coach was not to improve Sampras's ground strokes, but only to ensure that they didn't undermine his game. The path to championships was to concentrate on making his fabulous serve even better.

This isn't to say that addressing weakness is not important. If a worker is a poor listener, as I sometimes am, he should by all means know it and work on it. This involves awareness of the issue and identifying the triggers that set it off. But often the key to great success is to focus on people's outstanding Front of T-Shirt assets, whether design or math skills, and help them enhance these. This can help them develop from good to great.

Not everyone reading this book will be a CEO with the freedom and power to establish a coaching culture. Some people—most, in fact—work in companies where coaching is viewed as a sidelight which barely squeezes into job descriptions.

What to do then? Start small. Bring a junior employee under your wing. Start coaching. Then move to the whole team. Establish within that small group a culture of communication, goals, and feedback. The rest of the company may not catch on right away, but your team will become amazing. And that's a great start.

COACHING AT THE TOP

If you consider the design of the coaching scheme I've described, it flows down the org chart like tinsel on a Christmas tree, with everyone coaching the people who report to them. This flow is cyclical, since coaches gather feedback and performance data to improve their coaching. But there's one person who sits atop the company, with only the board of directors above. So who coaches the CEO?

The chief executive can gather all sorts of insights from fellow executives and direct reports, but a coach is a different animal. A coach can help set goals, attack weaknesses, bolster strengths. A coach can keep the dark secrets, help dig deeper to find their sources, and mold a response.

For this kind of relationship, a CEO usually has to look outside the company. Ask around. Most CEOs will probably end up at shops like CoachSource, Cambria Consulting, or CFAR (the Center for Applied Research). Those companies make executive coaching their business and have rosters of vetted professionals. In most cases, the firms will pick two or three potential coaches for a job. The CEO will meet them and choose one.

Then they go to work. In the most successful scenario, says Richard Levin, a coaching entrepreneur now at CFAR, the executive is looking for help, and has a goal to step it up in certain areas. "If that person has the appetite to grow and get stronger, that's ideal," he says.

The more problematic cases involve C-suite executives who are underperforming. In these cases, the board sends them to a coach to "fix" something. "That seldom works," Levin says, "unless they have an inner desire to change themselves as a leader."

Most coaching sessions begin with personality assessments, such as Hogan or PI, and interviews with the executive's closest circle of colleagues. Once the coaching sessions begin, Levin says, it's also important to establish metrics, so that progress can be measured. In my case, for example, I would confide to the coach that I have trouble listening. People talk, and I sometimes find my mind wandering. They notice. It's bad for morale and bad for my leadership because I'm not hearing what they say.

In such a case, he'd give me what he calls a "homework assignment" to interview a colleague and to engage in every word. Naturally, he would ask me in the next session how it went. But he'd also go beyond that, following up with people in my circles, asking for feedback on my listening. In this way, we would track my progress.

But like Pete Sampras's coach, Tim Gullikson, Levin also stresses the importance of focusing on the positive. "Where are you strong, and where could you be better?" he asks. "You have to play to those strengths."

Improvement, of course, is the greatest payoff from hiring a coach. But there are side benefits as well. Once chief executives see how much they benefit from the help, they'll be even more eager to establish a coaching culture in the company. Everyone can benefit from attention, accountability, and support.

NEXT STEPS

- To create an environment of openness and willingness to grow, kick-start coaching by sharing your Front of T-Shirt/Back of T-Shirt (FOT/BOT) with your team. (This addresses the logical question: If senior leadership is not actively working on "their stuff," why should anyone else?)
- Develop your reports' FOT/BOT jointly. Make this a quarterly check-in.
- Identify triggers for BOT issues. Give regular truthful, specific feedback as people gain on BOT goals.

Hiring

Picture three young professionals kibitzing about work over coffee. Two of them are in full-bellyaching mode, complaining about an angry boss, deadbeats who make too much money, passive-aggressive colleagues, miserly vacation schedules, and so on. The other person sits quietly. She doesn't have much to add to this misery. When they ask her about her job, she admits, almost apologetically, that she likes it. Her colleagues are supportive, she has chances to learn and advance, she finds purpose there.

In that one exchange, her company's hiring brand gets a boost. Two people emerge from the coffee shop with a positive impression of it. They may mention it to friends.

A week or two later, when the same trio meets again for coffee, the woman tells them about a job opening. Would either of them be interested?

At our company, we rely heavily on referrals, which are indispensable for luring glittering prospects toward a company.

A hiring brand is not something that can be built on its own, like an advertising campaign or customer relationship management software platform. It reflects the entire experience of working somewhere. The best way to build a hiring brand is simply to create a smart, friendly, and supportive workplace.

But some firms might need a kick start. Take a look at your company profile on a job and recruiting site, like Glassdoor. If there aren't a lot of reviews there, ask employees, both past and present, to post. Every review helps. Even if it's negative, it might point to a problem you can address. In that sense, you've created an important feedback loop.

A stellar hiring brand is essential for building dream teams. After all, the most valuable employees usually have the pick of the field. And given the choice, why would they go where people feel unhappy or stifled?

BUILDING A HIRING SYSTEM

Up to this point in the book, we've focused on aligning an enterprise and orienting it toward talent optimization. This involves matching skills and personalities to strategy, building dream teams, and continually enhancing them with coaching. Along the way, some of the people didn't fit, and others left. They're elsewhere, hopefully, as Happy Alumni.

Now we've reached the point where it's time to add new talent. Hiring the right people is fundamental to success. How exactly do you draw the right people to your door, and then decide which of them belongs on the team?

This is no time for winging it or willy-nilly decisions. That's talent roulette. It leaves the fate of the enterprise to chance.

For effective talent optimization, you need a formal and disciplined hiring system. Building one and implementing it is a bear, and it draws on the time and brainpower of much of the company—but it's essential. In the coming pages, I'll detail the hiring procedures we have developed at our company.

I look at our hiring regime as a subspecies in the genus of learning machines. It has many parallels to other optimization engines in the data economy, from the recommendation generator at Netflix to the bevy of machine-learning algorithms whirring away at the heart of Google search. All of these processes, including our own, measure and assess at every juncture. They also feature multiple feedback loops, so that they can see what works and what doesn't, and then recalibrate, eternally optimizing.

To be sure, our hiring system relies on human insights to a much greater degree than its automated cousins do. That's because our scale is vastly smaller. We concentrate on single individuals. What's more, we human beings, even with all of our biases and blind spots, continue to be experts at reading each other. Our insights must fit into the architecture of an analytics engine.

When embarking on a project like this, it's essential to have strong and steady support at the top. This is because optimized hiring is initially disruptive. In the early stages, it costs money and time. It can be maddening. You cannot launch this from the bowels of an HR department with wishy-washy support from the corner office. That will never work because it is bound to test the patience of everyone in the C-suite.

Indeed, it will be slower and more deliberate than they'd like, especially in the early stages. Sticking with the optimized approach often means going against the gut. It means resisting the temptation to fill a vacancy quickly with a candidate who looks pretty good—and instead waiting for someone great. It also means having the discipline to resist bypassing the system, even when an applicant has strong support in the C-suite.

Let me lead you through our hiring engine. For focus, let's imagine the company is in the market for a financial controller.

DEFINING PARAMETERS FOR THE JOB

The first step, long before reaching out to applicants, is to come up with a profile for the job. For this, we bring together three or four people. This includes someone from HR and, in our hypothetical case, someone from finance.

The ultimate goal is to replicate or even improve upon the brightest stars ever to hold the job at the company. What made those people remarkable? Did they have similar psychometric charts or job experiences? Were their cognitive scores in the range for that role? By sifting through the data (some of it anonymous to protect people's privacy), this group will piece together the model of a successful candidate. In this case, the behavioral profile of the ideal controller will likely trend toward patience and formality. This would put them into the Results & Discipline quadrant on the lower right, or lower left, Process & Precision. Candidates to the right of this chart are more likely to be hard drivers, while those on the left will focus more on the process, including its details and rules. Over time, these benchmark models get baked into templates.

The controller job, I should add, is fairly well defined in terms of skills and behavioral profile. Other jobs offer more wiggle room. You might think that a software engineer, similar to a controller, would focus on process. But we might come across a software engineer who's sky-high on extroversion and dominance and doesn't dwell much on the details. Such a person might not thrive in a coding job, but could have the vision and personality to lead a team or oversee the architecture for a new venture. The same goes for people building products. Some of them must focus on details. Others, from the Cultivating quadrant, are likely to be supportive team players, while you might need Explorers to dream up new products, or even new markets.

As I've mentioned, the job profile for candidates will feature a cognitive assessment. Cognitive scores are the most sensitive data in our company. For this reason, scores on these assessments are highly confidential. Only a very limited contingent at the company (which does not include me) has access to the results. Yet the numbers are extremely valuable. They track like no other metric to success. So in building the job profile, people with access to that data analyze the cognitive scores of people who have thrived in that job. They use them to establish a cognitive range. The cognitive score, it's important to note, should never be a singular variable disqualifier, because it picks up socioeconomic biases, including race and ethnicity.

The next step is to make sure that we're aligned on what this new hire will be doing. This might sound axiomatic. The controller will be monitoring the money coming in and going out and creating financial reports. But different constituencies within the company are likely to have conflicting ideas about exactly where this new hire will fit. The result is this kind of exchange:

"So I hear he's going to be working on taxes."

"Right, we need that."

"But I thought he was going to be working on the forensics of the Hong Kong acquisition. That's why his Cantonese was so important."

"Well . . . he can do that later . . ."

To steer clear of this kind of mess and to avoid false advertising to job applicants, we draw up a list of three tasks the manager will be expecting the new hire to focus on during the first 90 days on the job. This irons out disagreements before the hire and helps to harmonize the interview process. After all, if an applicant gets different visions from different managers, the logical assumption will be that we don't have our act together. For job applicants, it can (and should) flash an intense warning signal. When managers aren't in harmony, an employee who pleases one manager risks angering another. This can create enormous stress.

REACHING OUT

At this point, with the behavioral profile established, cognitive range set, and job duties agreed upon, we turn our sights outward. It's time to prepare the messaging for the job. This is crucial communication, a chance to entice the right candidates with what should be an exciting opportunity.

However, in many companies, the job description is an absolute snore. Many read as if lifted from a Commerce Department spreadsheet. Here's a typical example, this one for a job in Paramus, New Jersey:

> This includes general accounting and reporting, maintenance of the general ledger, analysis of accounts, monitoring accounts receivables, payables and cash . . .

I'm guessing your heart didn't skip a beat while reading that. Meaning no offense to my friends in finance, they're the ones responsible for most of the boring, plain vanilla job descriptions. This is because in a lot of firms, including most small to midsized ones, the HR operation reports to finance. That has its logic. The folks in finance put the new hires on payroll, set up their benefits and vacation time, and process their tax forms. From a purely logistical viewpoint, they're the ones who *handle* new hires. And for this reason, a lot of payroll systems include HR modules. Many give it away.

I've practiced selling The Predictive Index and have encountered finance people at every stage. I've seen how their needs and thinking dominate HR. When I ask if they're interested in data, the answer is almost always an enthusiastic yes. They *love* data. The challenge they face, though, is to focus on people as people. This involves appealing to their psychology, everything from their pathologies to their dreams. How does an HR team working under the finance department build a hiring brand or come up with exciting pitches? They often don't.

Writing a job description is vital and creative work. It's reaching out with language. In many ways, it's similar to coming up with a compelling pitch on a dating site. Looking for a controller, we might appeal to the dreams of a process-driven professional: Do you like building operational perfection? Of course, we'll also mention the fun, the teamwork, and the values of the company. It's a pitch. If you want honey bees, you need pollen.

Like many other aspects of this HR science, it starts with the intelligence and vision of human beings on our team. But technology can help. We have tools that can measure the effectiveness of job descriptions, how each of them fares, and how we can optimize them.

We also have a job-description analyzer. Using AI and natural-language processing, it identifies gender bias in the descriptions, while also identifying behavioral profiles most likely to be attracted to the position. This enables us to tune the ad. Companies such as Textio are developing systems with many of these features. In time, I predict, it will become as prevalent as spell-check.

For that single controller job, there is a vast field of potential job applicants. It includes not only every controller looking for a job but also those employed elsewhere. We put those job descriptions in advertisements. For some jobs, we employ headhunters.

But one of our central strategies is to leverage the smarts and social networks of our entire team. For this, we turn everyone into a recruiter and reward them for results. If someone steers a successful applicant our way, we pay a finder's fee, from $5,000 to $10,000. That might sound like a lot. But a star employee can make up that money within weeks. What's more, it's cheaper than hiring a headhunter. For a software engineer who makes $150,000 per year, a talent search firm will collect 20 percent, or $30,000. That's three times the reward we pay our team member. So it's a win-win, and we rely heavily on it.

(This comes with one important caveat: Referrals are bad for diversity, since more often than not people refer friends and former classmates from their own milieus. To add diversity, a company needs to adopt new strategies to spread the word.)

WINNOWING TO THE CHOSEN FEW

The mass of people applying for jobs are what we call the top of the funnel. The better the recruiting effort, the richer the blend at the top. But that's merely the beginning of a lengthy process. These people are about to pass through our hiring data machine. It features assessments and rounds of phone interviews, and it culminates in a Super Day, during which each finalist spends four hours at our offices, participating in structured interviews and carrying out a work assignment. At each of these steps, the candidates will be churning out data, which will lead us to the people we want to hire.

Naturally, if the people we hire don't thrive, we take that as feedback and look for ways to tweak the hiring process. Like their cousins in the internet economy, the data engines that power dream teams are forever learning and optimizing.

Returning to the hypothetical controller job we're trying to fill, let's imagine that our HR team has 10 candidates. The first step is to give each one of them a 20-minute introductory call on which the interviewer will describe the job and ensure that it fits with the candidate's career goals. They check that they're on the same page in terms of compensation, and also lay out the hiring process ahead. The next step, the applicant will learn, will involve taking two assessments, behavioral and cognitive.

Hearing this, a candidate might back out right away. This happens, but not often at our shop. After all, assessments are the heart of our business, and people who apply for these jobs are less likely to object to them. It's self-selection.

After they've completed these assessments, we put them through a software tool that matches them to the job template, in this case for controller. One of the candidates might score sky-high on cognitive, but the behavioral profile might show a focus on the big picture instead of on details and following rules. That person is probably not an ideal fit, at least for this job. Others test below the cognitive threshold.

I should add that while guarding the confidentiality of cognitive data, our team runs analyses comparing cognitive scores with performance in the different jobs. In fact, for some jobs, such as those dealing with greater complexity, we nudge up the cognitive threshold. The goal, after all, is to position people for success.

Our analysis of the test results might cull the group from 10 to 3. The next step for this reduced contingent is an in-depth phone interview with a manager who's an expert at the job. First, the interviewer must verify that candidates are who they claim to be on their résumés. We call that the "sanity check." The interviewer asks them to trace their career to date and to share their goals. This gives us grist for later conversations when we can drill down on specific examples. Interviewers also go over the candidates' needs and expectations for pay and benefits.

When it comes to compensation, our goal is to take it off the table by making it a nonissue. So, as I've mentioned, we pay well into the upper half of the industry average, aiming for the seventy-fifth percentile. (Other companies will set their pay bands according to needs. Elite consulting firms, for example, might push it higher than the seventy-fifth percentile, while certain retailers or manufacturers might be able to shoot lower and rely on training to lift performance.) The hope is that our pay is sufficient for the people we want, but we attract them with the culture and opportunities we offer. If someone is bent on getting top dollar, they'll probably jump quickly for more money elsewhere. These people are coin-operated and, usually, not a great fit for us.

During this lengthy interview, it's important to introduce the candidate to the culture of the company. In our case, this means hard work and lots of change. Those who flourish embrace our value system, THREADS. Hopefully, the interviewer comes away with the impression that the candidate is excited about working at a company with these values. Accepting them is essential, and it trumps any skill or expertise that an applicant may have, because our culture sustains the workplace.

Inevitably, candidates will ask how they fared on the assessments. They will have received the personality report, and the interviewer can go over it with them, answer questions, and discuss how their profile might fit the job.

Regarding the cognitive test, the conversation is a whole lot shorter. "Well, we're talking to you," the interviewer will say. This means that the candidate's cognitive results were sufficient for complexity of the role. No one needs to know more than that.

Some might argue that everyone has a right to the results of the cognitive test they've taken. If a cognitive assessment is so valuable, after all, shouldn't they be able to use that high number to lift their brand and open doors? In a word, no. Opening up scores could poison a workplace. They may contribute to a hierarchy, with entitled and certified brainiacs on top and the lower ranks weathering varying degrees of cognitive shaming.

For some jobs, the hiring company will want a record of strong skills. This is certainly true for law and accounting and for certain tech positions. But in our company, we look more for intelligence, drive, and cultural fit. Our company is engaged in building something new, so we're less interested in fitting skills into an established framework. The idea is that if we get the right team members on board, they'll be able to learn many of the skills they need. Every company (and position) will have its own hiring blend for skills versus culture.

After this second encounter, we analyze the assessments, skills, and feedback from the call and decide which candidates will come in for a Super Day. The final leg of the process involves a visit to the company with a string of structured interviews.

In the our early years, the Super Day was an exhausting marathon, featuring four hours of interviews, plus a work exercise that usually took about two hours. We later concluded that such an ordeal was too exhausting for the candidates, and a nightmare for those who went through it and got no job offer. So we split it up into two days.

First, before coming in for interviews, candidates do the exercise. For a controller position, they might be given the balance sheet and income statement for a company, real or fictitious. They have a limited time to study the documents and state in writing what they have learned about the company. In this case, the CFO follows up with a phone call to get a sense of the quality of their analysis (was it big picture or detailed?) and whether they seem to be a good match, given the culture.

The quality of the analysis accounts for 50 percent of the evaluation. The other 50 percent is awarded for how they think through the issues and the decisions they make along the way.

Marketing candidates might give a 15-minute presentation on the subject of their choosing. Here we want to see passion, energy, and storytelling, so the subject doesn't matter much. The question is whether the person can hold the room. One woman came in and sold the team on the quest that led her to what she deemed the best lobster roll in Boston. She nailed it, and later got the job.

Those who succeed in these exercises come in for Super Day. It features four hours of structured interviews, all of them following a schedule prepared by the hiring manager. I should note here that every interviewer has gone through interview training and practice sessions. This is not just to hone their interviewing skills, but also to set a standard. These are human beings, of course, so they'll naturally be different, but we want their judgments and scores to align. That's vital data.

Again, this is all part of the hiring learning machine, an ever-evolving system that draws input from lots of feedback loops. We want every stage of the process to be as fair and effective as possible. To this end, we score the interviewers. Some people are great at it. Others get better with practice, training, and feedback. For a few, it remains an elusive skill; they can contribute in many other ways.

The four hours usually involve five or six interviews, each with a different interviewer, and each interviewer with a specific concentration. One focuses on culture and THREADS. Others dig into the personality profile and ask questions about job history and vision. Some probe technical skills. Despite our best efforts to lighten it up, the process can be exhausting.

Sometimes, long before the candidate finishes the rounds of interviews, we have a clear consensus that the person is a keeper. In those cases, we reorient the later interviews. Instead of probing potential weaknesses or blind spots, the interviewer pivots to sell mode, evangelizing the experience, camaraderie, and opportunities at our company.

When they leave, we give each of the candidates an Amazon gift card to show our appreciation. We promise them a prompt response and ask them to fill out an evaluation of our application and interview process. Again, this provides more feedback data to help us refine our hiring engine.

As the Super Day comes to a close, each interviewer fills out a scorecard, which goes into our applicant tracking records. (It's important to get these into the system ASAP, so that people don't get a feel for what their boss thinks and adjust their views accordingly.) Later, they compare notes and discuss whether to hire the person. A central question: Would you want to work with this person, yes or no? Every person's scorecard is up on the screen, and each interviewer gets 90 seconds to talk about it. Disagreements are common, which is fine. They give us a chance to see different elements of a candidate. Usually, the manager emerges from this meeting with a clear idea of the candidate to hire.

Following the decision, we get in touch with those who did not get offers. We answer their questions and provide them with a blow-by-blow analysis of the process, explaining why they missed out. We tell many of them that we hope to see them again, and we often do. Again, treating these people well helps them, helps us, and boosts our hiring brand.

The timing in hiring can be extremely delicate. Say we have a solid candidate heading into his or her Super Day, but an even brighter prospect just beginning the process. In such a case, we do what we can to speed up the second candidate and slow down the first. This might mean postponing Super Day, if possible. But you can't make great hires cool their heels for more than 10 days. Every day of delay makes it more likely that they'll jump aboard another ship.

Analysis continues long after the applicant takes the job, feeding our learning machine for hiring. We look at the performance of the newly hired controller, and then use it to refine our model for the ideal in that job. If the employee doesn't work out, can we find clues, looking back, that might have predicted this? At the same time, we look at the interviewers and grade them. Did someone give this candidate five stars? If so, maybe that interviewer is more generous than average. It might be something that the system should allow for next time around.

Many companies, of course, bypass this data approach and focus on heuristics, or rules. Maybe they hire from certain colleges or business schools and are happy with the results. But sticking with a fixed formula usually means accepting the status quo and not questioning it, much less working to enhance it.

Unlike these static rules, a process built on data brings new insights. In baseball, to cite Billy Beane and his disciples once more, general managers eagerly drafted young talent for decades. History had taught them that the great stars in the game, from Babe Ruth to Willie Mays, tore up the competition in the Minor League and burst into Major League stardom in their early twenties, if not before. College players, by contrast, were already 22 or so when they began their journey. They were on a slower track.

Paul DePodesta, the Beane protégé who later moved to the Los Angeles Dodgers, looked at the numbers. He saw that college players made their way through the minors much faster than the younger high school recruits. College, in a real sense, was a minor league. And the college game featured a host of new data tools that provided scouts with advanced analytics on prospects, from the velocity on batters' line drives to the spin rate on pitchers' curveballs.

Studying this data and projecting the financial impact, DePodesta pivoted away from high school players—and the rest of the baseball industry followed suit. As recently as 1998, baseball teams drafted equal numbers of high school stars and college stars, with each group at about 48 percent of the total. Twenty years later, the draft was dominated by university players. They made up 76 percent of the total.* By studying feedback data, Paul DePodesta had, in effect, tweaked baseball's hiring algorithm.

EXECUTIVE HIRING

Every hire is important, but a few are critical. I'm talking about executive positions, where hiring the right person can be transformational. The right head of product might lead the team toward an innovation that sprouts a lucrative new business. With savvy market moves, a brilliant chief financial officer might free up money for a prized acquisition. On the other hand, picking the wrong person for these jobs can send the enterprise off the rails.

These are huge hires, and they demand a serious and disciplined process. Before I walk you through ours, remember one important point: don't hurry. The risk of picking the wrong person is too great. If you have a key position that's open, fill it with someone on an interim basis. Maybe the chief operating officer can run the product team for a few months. A temporary CFO can keep finances in line. Give yourself the time you need to find the person you need for the permanent post.

The first step in this star hunt is to define the job. It might sound obvious. A head of product runs the team that builds stuff. But there are several flavors of that job, and there's an excellent chance that not everyone on the executive team agrees on which type is needed.

We start with a thought experiment. Of all the people in the world, who would be ideal in the role? No one is off the

_____

* https://www.baseballamerica.com/stories/draft-system-has-pushed-teams
-to-pick-more-college-players/.

board. We can consider CEOs of competitors, Chinese super-stars who don't speak English, dead people. The idea is to come up with a type.

For the head of product job, for example, we might con-sider David Cancel, founder of Drift. He's a product visionary who can turn a team toward a North Star. He's not available, but that's not the point. Is that the kind of person we want? Or are we looking for a logistical whiz who can turn our product development into a turbocharged machine? This is a key dis-cussion because it helps to align the team around the right qualities for the role.

Once we figure out the kind of person we're looking for, we consider everyone in our sphere, including people with whom we have worked. Is there anyone in that large cohort who dis-plays those qualities? It doesn't necessarily have to be in the same field.

When we were looking to fill a senior product position, we thought about an extremely gifted manager we'd worked with at LEDCO, our manufacturing turnaround outside of Detroit. His name was Jay Shaw. He worked in hardware, not software. But his qualities were relevant. He had a gift for distilling the concepts people were looking for into design. He would ask them to draw their ideas on the whiteboard.

"But I'm not good at drawing," they'd often say.

"That's OK," Jay would tell them. "I'm really good at inter-preting bad drawings. Go ahead and draw." So they'd start, and Jay would draw behind them, saying, "Do you mean this?" In this way, his team developed great products.

Looking at the job as a puzzle to be assembled, we now had an important piece. The candidate should have some of Jay Shaw's qualities. These are difficult things to write into a job description, but at least we had the idea.

We discussed it with other stakeholders, including top executives. And we launched another thought experiment.

Was there anyone within our 165-person team who exhibited some of these elements? Who would we put in the role if we had only our own team to consider? Maybe the best person for the job wasn't senior enough or lacked a few of the necessary skills. But this thought process added context and clarity to the role. (This exercise also has side benefits: You might now look at this junior employee in a new light and take steps to prepare her for a leadership role.)

A template for the job was coming together, and we could begin to fill out the job description. But there were still questions to consider. Did we need someone who had done the job before? What was our tolerance for risk?

Many companies hire executive search firms without taking these steps to align the team around their ideal candidate. Often, in these cases, savvy headhunters will spur alignment by presenting a couple of second-tier candidates early in the process. These amount to test runs, but they spark necessary discussions. What did you like or dislike about the candidates? Why are they wrong for the job? What exactly *is* the job?

Whether prodded by headhunters or through an internal process like ours, alignment about the nature of the job and the type of candidate required is essential. It goes into the job description. At that point, you're ready to use whatever methods are at hand, whether personal networks, ads, or headhunters, to bring in candidates.

Certain services guide executive teams through this exercise. Topgrading, for example, is a rigorous methodology. It features long sessions to define the job, a series of highly structured interviews, and exhaustive trawling through each candidate's life and career stories. It also includes background checks to certify their claims. In my experience, these procedures function as a level of quality control, the equivalent of a due diligence audit. Where they come up short, however, is in highlighting a candidate's weak points.

We've developed our own procedure for this, and it's a cinch to implement. On our calls to references, we naturally find lots of people eager to sing the candidate's praises. And that's fine. But we tell them that we will not even consider their input unless they give us several of the person's weak points. The idea, we tell them, is not to sink the candidacy, but instead to provide guidance. After all, if we're going to start a career development path with this person, we have to know what to work on.

This often provides rich insights, prime Back of T-Shirt material. And it often syncs with the other assessments we do, including the personality charts. The key is not to hire a candidate without warts. We all have them. But it's essential to know where they are from the get-go.

The hiring, from our point of view, doesn't truly conclude until they've been on the job for three months, or 90 days. At that point, we check with the new hires on their progress toward a host of target goals. And among ourselves we ask a pointedly simple question: If we had to do it again, would we hire this person?

This might sound like useless second-guessing. But it generates data for our hiring machine. If the hire isn't working out, was there some piece of data we ignored, a sign that was there, but not in bold relief? If so, should we tweak the system to make those more visible?

At the same time, our recruiters are keenly focused on those 90-day reviews because their compensation is tied to it. They get rewarded not just for hires but successful ones. It's at 90 days when we make this determination.

Sometimes, despite all of this effort, we see after 90 days that one of these crucial hires is underperforming. European companies pay special attention during these early months. Many have only a six-month window to fire new employees, and after that their jobs are strongly protected by law, so it makes sense to monitor new hires closely in the early months. In extreme cases, a mistake can lead to 40 years of misery for both the employee and the rest of the team.

Even though we don't have such strong labor laws in America, it makes sense to follow this thinking. We do. When someone falls short by one measure or another, whether in performance or cultural fit, it's clear pretty early as long as you're paying attention. If the new hire isn't meeting expectations after three months, and fails to address it by six months, it's time to act. With junior employees, we can often move them to another team or department and give them a second chance. Someone stumbling in product might thrive in sales, especially if she's high on dominance. But executive hires have no lateral moves to make. If they're underperforming, they're probably dragging down an important piece of the company. Patience is a luxury few companies can afford when a top executive is missing the mark. It spells slow death. Better to move on.

On the bright side, you'll already have alignment on the defined job, and most likely a host of vetted candidates eager to fill it.

NEXT STEPS

- The best time to create a good hiring brand is 20 years ago, so do not wait another day. This will take time to build and deliver for you.
- Develop a rigorous system, incorporating training, standard scoring rubrics, and feedback loops.
- Define each job—and make sure your team is aligned on it—and create achievement benchmarks for the first six months.

Onboarding

A bountiful fruit basket appears at the new employee's front door. Ideally, it brims with the most delicious fruits for the season, whether it's perfect pears, crunchy apples, or peaches at their sweetest. In the scenario, as we envision it, the surprised family members bring the basket inside and tear open the card. "It's from your new company!" they say.

Thus begins our onboarding process. The idea of the fruit basket is to reach out not just to the new "PIoneer," but to his or her entire household. Hopefully, they'll identify the company with the surprise of opening the door to the fruit basket and the taste of fresh cherries or nectarines.

Our onboarding process lasts for an entire year. But the first weeks are much more intense, and crucial for getting new team members started on the right foot. Like so much else in building dream teams, success hinges on a combination of knowledge and imagination. What do we know about each new PIoneer, and how can we use that to imagine what their experience must be like on day one at our company? Once we can put ourselves in their shoes, it's a matter of making everything as pleasant and effective as possible; in short, optimizing their onboarding.

The first days and weeks at a company mark the experience, for better or worse, so we take great pains to make it as clear as possible to the new hires that we have their backs. This means understanding when they screw up, as everyone does at one point or another. It means assuming that they meant to get it right when they show up at a meeting late and flustered, when they neglect to include their manager on a calendar invite, when they forget their key card and find themselves locked out of the bathroom. These things happen.

The onboarding process launches well before the new hire's first day. At about the same time the fruit basket arrives, the hiring manager receives a link to a flowchart tool that lays out the to-do list on a calendar. (We use Asana, but there are loads of options.) The first steps, tagged ASAP, are to reach out to the new member and get the other team members to send messages and connect with the new colleague on LinkedIn. The manager should also start to set up an Asana board for the new hire.

The new hires, meanwhile, receive a welcome email with details about what awaits them in their first week. This mail includes a link that leads them through the PI personality assessment. It provides them with their profile, along with some analysis. It also introduces them to the psychometric charts of their fellow team members (so they won't be surprised on day one when the High Dominance/Low Patience colleague pushes her ideas more energetically than the others, and drums her fingers during a discussion of details).

In the year after we bought the business, we made sure to pack people's first week or two to the gills. They learned about the company and its mission and were schooled on benefits. At the same time, they plunged into work with their team. We were welcoming them to a fast-moving enterprise, as advertised.

We were overdoing it, we soon heard. We learned from feedback that while the experience was warm and friendly, it was also overwhelming. "I felt like I was treading water and gulping it down at the same time," one of our colleagues recalls. "You're trying to learn how to be a person at this company that moves fast, and also adjusting to your job that moves fast."

So we slowed it down. For starters, we told hiring managers to tap the brakes. Often, they're struggling to backfill a position and are eager to get the new hires up and running ASAP. A good number would pound new reports' in-boxes with advance job information so that they could be productive from day one. Many of the new hires, though, are busy finishing up their old jobs, or taking a week between jobs to decompress. The last thing they need from us is job stress, so we restrain the managers, telling them to hold off until the PIoneers start work.

Much of the onboarding process is designed to make the hiring manager look like the most thoughtful and compassionate boss in the world. This is best for the relationship with the employee. It also boosts company morale. The central point is to help them anticipate the new employee's needs and concerns, and to deliver help. This may sound like a press release, but like the rest of talent optimization, it's anchored in the ABCs of smart management. Employees are much more likely to be engaged if they have a good relationship with their manager. And engaged employees are far and away more productive. So if providing a runway in their early days helps to produce this result, why scrimp on it?

The essence of the onboarding philosophy is for managers, during this period, to focus on what the new hires need to be successful, and much less on short-term production. Consider, for example, that person's first day. One of the most disheartening experiences when starting a new job is to click open the calendar and see . . . nothing, every day a blank. For many, the empty calendar stirs fears that they should be doing something, but they don't know exactly what. In many workplaces, newbies spend anxious hours sitting at their desks pretending to be busy, hoping no one notices, while awaiting instructions. These are the worries that interfere with their sleep and diet. They start off the new job with a thud.

So, a week before the PIoneer's first day, one of the tasks that pops up on the Asana board for the hiring manager is to fill up the person's calendar. This means setting up lunches and recurring meetings, and scheduling one-on-ones with colleagues inside and outside the group.

On that first day, each person meets his or her "New Hire Buddy." This is someone from outside of their department, a friendly colleague who will gladly answer "dumb questions." They might be about vacations, jargon they don't understand, the etiquette surrounding snacking on the job. Maybe he or she can introduce them to a helpful person on the tech team. The New Hire Buddy checks in at the end of the first week, and then a couple more times in the first month.

Having a New Hire Buddy is even more important during times of crisis, such as the COVID-19 pandemic. Not long ago, we learned through this program that a new hire was stuck in a poisonous relationship and was drinking during the day to cope with it. This was a significant issue, and we were able to get the person help.

Early on in developing our onboarding process, we saw that what we had in place, including the New Hire Buddies, wasn't enough. From feedback, it became clear to us that before starting their jobs, the new hires needed a foundation course on the business: the company, its strategy and its core product, the personality assessment.

The orientation program we developed takes a week, and each month a new class of hires goes through it. The week includes everything from our core THREADS values to the location of the bathrooms. On their first day, I meet with the new hires. I generally give them the backstory of the company, how my business partner and I happened upon the assessments and ended up buying the company that created them. In effect, I tell them, we're co-CEOs, even though I have the title. (This is intended to show a hint of vulnerability.) In the same vein, I tell them that while Daniel and I are shareholders in the company, we do not own it. The board of directors oversees and regulates what we do. In that sense, we too have bosses.

During these first meetings I outline for new hires the future of the industry, as we see it, and the path to talent optimization. I stress our mission—Better Work, Better World—and make the point that openness is a crucial component. To illustrate the point, I tell them that they can ask me absolutely anything. Most of them, since it is early days and they're talking to the CEO, resist the temptation to ask me about my greatest fear. (It's failing.)

Tuesday of orientation week is what we call "MBA in a day." This includes meeting with company leaders, clients, and partners and learning about the business, how all the pieces and relationships fit together. Then they have a two-day deep dive into the framework of our behavioral assessments—what the assessments can tell us, and how they guide our efforts. On Friday, we school them on talent optimization: the theory, assessments, and what it means for the future of work. Hopefully, these sessions provide them with a deep understanding of the product and customer use cases, giving them a sharper perspective on what their work is about. Each one gets certification as a Talent Optimizer.

As new PIoneers go through this training, a logical question will often pop up. If the entire business is predicated on customizing the work experience for each individual, is that happening to me now?

The answer is yes. We calibrate the onboarding to each employee's personality. Let's say that we determine that new team members need, on average, three weeks, or 120 hours, to learn processes and get up to speed. Those who score high in Dominance, like me, will want to have a hand in designing their own onboarding. So a hiring manager might give them an idea of what they need to learn, and whom they should be meeting with, and then let them figure out how to get it done.

Those high in extroversion will want to interact with people, so we don't put them in front of too many videos. Instead, we encourage them to meet colleagues and debrief them in person. Introverts, by contrast, might prefer to consume the information on video, away from the hubbub.

We keep in mind the different personalities when organizing our welcoming ceremonies. These take place during new hires' first month. They learn about it when an invitation to a meeting pops up on their calendars. In a devilish twist, the start time is about 10 minutes late, so by the time they show up to an all-hands meeting, everyone is already seated. The new PIoneers then walk up the aisle as everyone cheers.

Each one is then introduced and asked to tell their new colleagues one fun fact about their life. Maybe they're rock climbers or play lead guitar in a heavy metal band. Maybe they can solve Rubik's Cube in 14 seconds. Whatever it is, the fun fact provides colleagues with a connection point. While washing hands at adjoining sinks, someone might not remember the newbie's name, but can still ask: What was the name of that ant caviar you ate in Mexico?

This welcoming event is delightful for many, but it can push all kinds of buttons for introverts, so we help prepare them. We tell them in advance to come up with a fun fact because people low on Extroversion often prefer to gather their thoughts before speaking. And then we make sure that they have plenty of company for their celebratory stroll down the aisle.

GETTING DOWN TO WORK

At this point, it may sound like work is something of an afterthought during the onboarding process. Not the case. If we look through the eyes of new hires, the actual job is their greatest interest and concern. Success, they know, is key to their happiness, career, prosperity, even the quality of their sleep. Having a supportive manager and team members helps, of course. But the biggest source of concern for most boils down to three central questions: What is expected of me? What is the timeline? How will I be judged for the results?

At a lot of companies, managers mistakenly signal support for the new hire by leaving these questions unanswered. "Oh, don't worry," they say. "You'll figure it out." This approach is intended to relieve pressure on new hires. In fact, it accentuates it because it leaves them in the dark. This lack of precision, I suspect, is often grounded in laziness. Managers haven't thought in great detail about what the new hire will produce. Instead, they'll wait and see. Good hires produce a lot. Bad ones fail.

At our company, we map out targets for each new employee—spelling out what they're expected to achieve within three, six, and nine months. At each juncture, the manager fills out a performance review, marking the progress on each target, and then sits down with the new hire to review the results. If someone has fallen short in the first trimester, what help do they need to succeed? More resources or training? Is there a problem on the team? The message is that their success is our success.

This process might sound like a lot of pressure, but it actually provides reassurance during the year of the onboarding process. It dispels doubts. Most people come away from these meetings knowing that they're doing fine. And those who aren't on track aren't simply left to fail, feeling dread all the while. They get help. In either case, nothing should be a surprise between the employee and the manager because communication is constant.

At the end of the year, new employees face their first full 360 review, with input from managers and colleagues. Onboarding is over for this class of hires, but many others are going through the process, at least a few every month. At a fast-growth company, first-year employees make up a large contingent, and onboarding is a big part of the company's day-to-day business. It's focused on developing its most important asset: its people.

As long as growth keeps up, the cycle of hiring, onboarding, and coaching rolls on. It can feel, during these heady times, as though you finally have things figured out. But as we'll see in the next chapter, the comfy status quo can be upended from one day to the next—which brings on a host of new challenges.

NEXT STEPS

- ◎ Get personally involved with the onboarding process on day one. This is your culture, and first impressions are *huge*.
- ◎ Assign an empathetic hiring buddy for each new hire. These are ambassadors of the culture.
- ◎ Send a gift or a handwritten note to every new hire as soon as you make the offer. (Depending on the size of your company, this should come from the CEO or, at least, the hiring manager.)
- ◎ Use psychometric tools to adapt to the new hire's learning style. It's an investment in their success—and in that of company.

Crisis

Global markets crash. A hurricane wrecks a supply chain. Riots topple an elected government. A pandemic shuts down an economy.

We learn from disasters, and our natural tendency is to erect defenses against the most recent since they're the freshest in our memory. But there's an excellent chance that the next crisis, whether natural disaster, financial collapse, or war, won't be like the last one. So the trick is to extract learnings from rough times that are foundational to crisis itself.

A crisis amounts to a stress test for an entire group of people. A team is at risk, but the response of that team is also the key to survival. The response requires discovery, innovation, and teamwork. This process can sink an enterprise, but it can also transform it—and much depends on how the team is managed, repurposed, and inspired.

As a sailor, I look at crises from the perspective of a ship captain. We start out with a crew, one that fits the ship's original design and mission. But as we head into a vicious storm, that mission is transformed. Survival depends on this pivot.

The new mission requires a shift in strategy, as well as a reconfigured deployment of the crew.

On these occasions, I often think of a poem by Sir Francis Drake. The sixteenth-century privateer (considered by some to be a pirate) was one of the supreme navigators of his time. He supposedly penned his famous poem shortly before embarking on his greatest and riskiest venture, the circumnavigation of the globe. In my favorite stanza, he wrote:

> Disturb us, Lord, to dare more boldly,
> To venture on wider seas
> Where storms will show your mastery;
> Where losing sight of land,
> We shall find the stars.

The most daunting challenges are also opportunities. It is when facing crises, whether random or self-inflicted, that captains and crews discover and define themselves. They're pushed above and beyond their established routines.

KEN CHENAULT'S ADVICE

Early on in the COVID-19 pandemic, one of our venture investors, General Catalyst, offered to put us in touch with Ken Chenault, a partner at the firm. Chenault had served as CEO of American Express for more than a decade, and had learned firsthand about managing through the most tumultuous times. He had weathered an intense travel crisis following the attacks of September 11, 2001. That was the core of American Express's business. But AmEx was also a banking company. And seven years later, following the 2008 collapse of Lehman Brothers, it survived a global financial freefall. Ken Chenault knew all about crises.

He gave us the following keys, all of them crisis-agnostic.

1. Honesty: Communication must be prompt, steady, and brutally honest. "You can't whitewash this," he said. The team must understand the stakes involved and the looming challenges.

2. Risk: Make it clear that the threat is existential. It is likely to snuff out a number of companies. Vigorous and painful action might be the only way to save the team—and it won't be everyone.

3. Story: The communication must fit into a narrative, one that leads eventually to a brighter future. Chenault wasn't talking about a Pollyanna vision, in which everything quickly gets better. In fact, too much optimism can backfire. If things don't improve quickly, the leader loses the trust of the people. It breeds cynicism.

4. Purpose: The team has a mission, a *why*. Fighting through this difficult time is the only way to achieve it.

Communication is key. That's been true for all of human history. But how to map out the change and manage the response of the team?

THE TOOL KIT

When crisis hits, it's a good idea to consult the same personality assessments that were used to build the status quo. But this time you employ them to reshape the enterprise.

A crisis calls for two different missions. The first is survival. This involves making it through the six months of the most intense and threatening stage of the crisis, whatever its nature. This is the storm. If the company is a ship, it needs the right crew in place.

But there's also a second mission to focus on: the enterprise following the crisis. It must establish a niche for itself in a reshaped landscape. This may be a year or 18 months away. What will the company look like at this stage? What talent will you need for it?

It's useful here to return to the Competing Values Framework. Consider a consulting company. During the good times, its collection of talent—the dots on the chart—seems to fit its needs and mission. Its Stabilizing quadrant, in the lower left, has a solid contingent of rule-based perfectionists. The top salespeople, meanwhile, populate the lower right Producing quadrant. But most of its dots are in the upper left, the Cultivating quadrant, or Teamwork & Employee Experience. Consulting, by its very nature, teems with Cultivators.

But in the current crisis the consulting market has collapsed. The company's survival strategy is to push vigorously into software. The idea is to reduce its reliance on people and embed a chunk of their knowledge into a tech offering.

The top executives think they have enough cash to make it through the storm, although they must be leaner. In the meantime, they figure they must cut costs by 40 percent to subsist.

Where to cut? As a company plows from consulting into software, it's likely to need a different mix of people: more from the Stabilizing quadrant, fewer Cultivators. Part of the analysis is to take a look at that contingent of Cultivators. How many of them have skills that fit the design of the rebuilt company?

In this case, the psychometric tests serve a targeting function. They illuminate the cohort on which to focus. But that analysis quickly extends far beyond that test to their performance. Here, the 2x2 chart (see Figure 6.1), mapping the combination of Performance and Engagement, can be extremely useful. Again, the employees are represented by dots, but this time, arranged qualitatively. The ones in the upper-right quadrant, both high performing and engaged, are stars—keepers. Their counterparts in the lower left corner, Contaminators, are both low performing and disengaged. To put it brutally, that's the first place to look for cuts. No more than one reclamation project, if that.

You might think that a well-designed and well-run company would be identifying Contaminators all along, either helping them find their groove or sending them off as Happy Alumni. That's what I've been preaching. However, I've found that if a company has been faring well and growing, it's likely to have become lax. You're less inclined to fire underperformers when you're busy hiring and the numbers are good.

Although the 2x2 is useful, it leaves many questions unanswered. To make these difficult decisions, the annual 360s are a rich resource. They include manager and colleague reports, and the employee's detailed plan on how to address development and improve in areas of weakness.

This culling process can get political. Managers are committed to their teams, and they battle each other to save the jobs on their side. Decisions often rise to the top executive team. They're the referees and arbiters. The entire process is miserable. Managers are angry. Worse, esteemed colleagues are walking out the door.

But this should not come as a surprise. Honest communication from the get-go should let everyone know exactly what the company is facing and why the action is being taken. Perhaps the survivors will agree to take pay cuts and, thus, save more jobs. This is a discussion to have early on.

In any case, some people will be leaving. It should be made clear to them that they're appreciated, as friends and colleagues, and that, hopefully, some of them will be able to return when the storm is past. All of them should leave with the most generous possible severance. It's only fair to them, but also a sign to the rest of the workforce that they, too, are respected and cared for as people.

One way to burn this respect during a crisis is to call upon the heavyweight of assessments: cognitive. This could be tempting. Cognitive scores, after all, are more predictive of success than the others. So when the future of the company is at stake, you might think, why not use it? If the company needs to shrink, doesn't it make sense to start with those who rank in the lowest decile of cognitive ability?

This is a dangerous idea, one that could poison the entire workplace. While it is true that cognitive tests are useful for turnarounds—when the workforce needs dramatic change—they are not recommended for downsizing because they create enormous cultural damage. In this context, they are like chemotherapy. Even when chemo works, it kills other cells and tissue and causes nausea. The introduction of cognitive assessments into this already fraught drama breeds hierarchy, fear, and shame. For a downsizing enterprise in crisis, morale is already tenuous. It needs to be propped up, not pummeled. At the end of the day, an enterprise's survival hinges on a cohesive and hardworking team.

GAUGING THE MOOD

The ship has made it through the early stages of the storm. It's still afloat, more compact and with a smaller crew. The refitting is done. Now it's time to focus on operations during a crisis. Often, after the explosion of a crisis and the tumultuous early days, with layoffs and furloughs, people are frazzled. Some overwork, others feel like crashing. Some are depressed. A few might start drinking too much.

It's vital to get a grip on the changing dynamics and the mood. After all, getting people the help they need is impossible if you don't know how they're doing. In addition to encouraging lots of frank communication, it makes sense to survey the entire company. During the pandemic, we carried out engagement surveys every four months. You don't want to overload people with such surveys. But during times of crisis, things change fast and so do moods, including anxiety and frustration. There are other pulsing and polling tools, even the colorful mood buttons you see when coming out of airport lavatories. Any intelligence on how your team is faring is valuable.

INFINITE VERSUS FINITE

Through the difficult months of crisis, it's only natural to fixate on questions of time. When will it end? Two more months? By summertime? Will we be back to something approaching normal by next year?

The focus is on the end. The crisis is viewed and treated as a finite event. Bestselling author and consultant Simon Sinek distinguishes between two perspectives on life and business: finite and infinite. It's vital, especially during a crisis, to keep both in mind.

A crisis is brimming with finite challenges—slashing expenses, winnowing the workforce. It's a process. You get through it. Many of these finite challenges demand immediate attention and strong focus. If a bank demands payments three weeks from tomorrow, the whole team is caught up in a finite challenge.

The infinite exists in a different dimension. It is tied to values and vision. It provides purpose. In Drake's voyage, a storm represents a finite challenge, but the sailors get through the storm to pursue their mission. That's the *why*, and it transcends time. In their case, it was to circumnavigate the globe and bring glory to England (and steal Peruvian gold from Spanish galleons while they were at it).

It's important throughout the crisis to keep the infinite vision in sight. Team members won't be pondering and discussing it all the time. This is a crisis, not a retreat. But it has to be there, understood and communicated. That way, all the pain they're going through has a purpose. There's a reason to survive. And a big part of it, if it's a dream team, is to keep working with each other. They've built something together, and they don't want to let it go. That motivation is infinite.

TURNING ON THE LIGHTS

Each crisis is different, and each demands a different strategy and approach. It's not just a matter of honest communication and building trust. A crisis also calls for innovation. The challenges push our brains into overdrive. As we exchange ideas, we pool our minds and multiply our intense problem-solving flow. Sometimes junior colleagues step up, breaking hierarchies, and push new concepts. The path out of crisis, whether personal or corporate, almost always leads to discovery.

Brighter days will come. And this raises the next challenge: how and when do you turn the lights back on and return to a hiring mode?

NEXT STEPS

- Identify for the entire team the challenges, the pathway to success, and the assumptions you're making. Articulate the metrics you are watching and the gambles you are taking.
- Lead by making bigger sacrifices at the most senior level.
- Develop a narrative tracing the way through the crisis, and emerging (if possible) even stronger.
- Use crises to rethink and remake the company for the future.

The Future

E ver since the introduction of the internet as a mass medium in the 1990s, futurists have been predicting a wholesale migration from physical offices to virtual ones. For years, that vision—dazzling to some, terrifying to others—remained elusive. Through the first two decades of the twenty-first century, office buildings continued to boom because there was a real benefit to bringing people together physically. After all, we human beings are social animals. Our encounters, whether in the lunch line or at adjoining sinks in the bathroom, are much more likely than videoconferences to spark serendipitous ideas and connections. What's more, the virtual experience was often suboptimal and, in many cases, painful.

As the pandemic of 2020 shuttered offices around the world, it brought about this long-delayed vision of virtual workplaces. By this time, video technology had advanced, which made days of Zoom meetings possible, if tiresome. Collaboration platforms like Slack and Box became ubiquitous.

Those apps are like the first spring crocuses poking up through the snow. Many other services, while still on the fringe, offer and blend conferencing, collaboration, and analytics, much of it buttressed by AI.

Consider simulated offices. On Sophya, a Harvard-bred startup, the people working from home appear in a simulation of the office. You can see people's avatars scattered through the virtual space. Some chat with colleagues in the coffee area, amid the potted palms. Others are seated in the conference room with the product team. In this scenario, a colleague working from her home in Brockton, Massachusetts, might see my avatar sitting alone in my office, perhaps with a green light to signal that I'm open to visits. She could knock on my virtual door, and then, using the video app, we could be talking face-to-face. Naturally, platforms like Sophya provide all the tools you'd expect, from meetings and scheduling to transcription of spoken conversations and translations, if necessary—in short, everything computers can do.

It's anyone's guess whether simulations based on real office layouts will prevail. Maybe a more appealing or efficient alternative will take root, one which has little or no resemblance to the physical office. Perhaps many of us will choose to keep going into the office, where we can see and interact with our colleagues without the help of technology. We don't know.

But one thing that's certain is that computers will be transmitting and recording more of our behavior at work. The tools and methods we relied on during the pandemic won't go away. No matter which platforms we choose, in physical or virtual settings, the machinery around us (and in our pockets) is sure to be recording, transmitting, and sharing ever more of our words, actions, and relationships. We will be generating petabytes of new behavioral data. And that ever-growing trove will fuel the continuing advance of talent optimization.

This is how data economies advance. An industry first figures out how to optimize with the data on hand. Then it casts about for new sources of data. Moneyball's Billy Beane, as we saw, started with traditional statistics that would have been familiar to Babe Ruth: runs, walks, on-base percentage. The industry has since surrounded the game with so many layers of sensors that managers can now yank a starting pitcher when the spin rate on his curveball dips to a certain threshold.

So which calculations will companies be able to make in coming years? Here's a small sampling:

- Which employees, based on sentiment analysis of their words, are the most upbeat?
- Who is the dominant personality in the sales marketing team? How do the interactions change when he's not around?
- Which social connections appear to be most productive (or toxic)?
- Who interrupts the most?
- Who are the best listeners?

I could go on. A host of new services will attempt to build businesses around these data streams, whether for hiring or team building. Some of these data services will succeed. Many will not. But through this process, the workplace will become an ever greater laboratory.

This future is already taking shape. For sales and marketing, for example, a startup called Gong.io captures spoken and written words from sales calls. It puts them through an AI engine that analyzes the words, the tone, the percentage of time each salesperson listens, how many laughs they generate, and so on. By focusing on the patterns of the top performers, the program can generate templates for best practices, what works and what doesn't.

A New York startup called BrightHire is out to do much the same for the murky interviewing process. The service helps interviewers organize their questions and priorities, even prompting them when necessary. This can help cut down on the maddening randomness of interviews, providing data that can be compared.

This type of app also cuts down on bias. It might take note, for example, when an interviewer, attempting to establish rapport with a Chicago-based candidate, strikes up a conversation about the Cubs. The app will discourage such detours, which could bias the interviewer toward baseball fans (and maybe even against Chicago baseball fans who root for the White Sox).

A number of startups offer to sift through the publicly available data of employees and job applicants to gather insights. These are the early days of this technology, and its first commercial applications are sure to raise red flags. A Los Angeles company called Fama, for example, has developed an AI tool to spot signs that an employee or prospect could poison the workplace. It hunts for unwelcome behaviors, such as signs of violence or racism on social networks.

The possibilities for this type of analysis are near limitless—but so are the risks. By scraping social data and scrutinizing online photos, companies could spot signs of problem drinking, drug use, and political extremism. In future iterations, these platforms might highlight happiness, healthy relationships, curiosity, and creativity.

Anyone using these snoopy tools, though, should keep the risks in mind. The coming surge of behavioral data, like that in healthcare, advertising, and on social networks, will raise all kinds of privacy issues. And this will lead to pain, in reputation and in the courts, if the analysis is carried on surreptitiously. Secrecy will result in liability.

Further, algorithmic analysis can get things wrong. Human biases, for example, are embedded in even the most sophisticated software systems. Say an AI is programmed to recognize neighborhoods where a lot of people buy illegal drugs, and then associates those neighborhoods with risk. Could that count against a job applicant who happens to live there?

It's better to look at this data revolution from the opposite perspective, as an opportunity to develop good will. It's essential to be clear with team members about what is being measured, why, and who will have access to the information. If they don't buy in, and if this trust isn't established, all of those fancy surveillance tools will be picking up distressing patterns: falling engagement, growing negativity, and, eventually, churn.

Some players, inevitably, will stumble into this future, undermining employees' and customers' goodwill. And certain vendors will no doubt make extravagant promises and hawk digital snake oil. This occurs at every stage of technological advance. Each failure and each scam feeds the skeptics.

The companies that figure it out will advance in talent optimization and leap ahead in productivity and innovation. Some of these will also establish themselves as cultural champions and enviable places to work.

This future isn't really a choice. It will be nearly impossible for companies to turn away from the next stage of the data economy while, at the same time, holding onto their platinum hiring brands. This is because their more advanced competitors will be outpacing them and devouring their markets. Companies in such weakened positions, no matter how warm and transparent the culture, cannot last long.

So how do you position yourself for this future? You begin by following the principles of talent optimization, which I've laid out in this book. By assessing and analyze people—their personalities, emotional intelligence, engagement, and more—an enterprise embarks on a path of continuous learning. With this, it starts to build its HR data engine, which features layer upon layer of feedback loops that direct talent along the optimal course.

Companies that adapt these techniques to hire, design, and coach will be off and running in the HR data economy.

• • •

Structural challenges also lie ahead, and will grow increasingly urgent. With the rise of AI and ever faster data networks, there will be ever greater levels of expertise on call. This intelligence might come from a machine or from a human expert. In either case, it raises a thorny question: how many experts will you need as full-time employees?

Consider the question from the experts' own perspective. How many of them will want to belong to a team, buy into a mission, and sell their services by the year? Some will, no doubt, but not all by a long shot. Experts will be extremely valuable. And a good number of them might find that they fare better by selling their services in the gig economy, by the minute or the problem solved.

So whom do we hire? If we return for a minute to Billy Beane, his small-market baseball team could not afford superstars. He had to look for undervalued talent and then train it up. The economics of expertise is going to push most of us in the same direction. Many of the AI savants and visionaries of software architecture are going to be prohibitively expensive, the equivalent of signing Mookie Betts, or, in soccer, Leo Messi, as free agents.

The troves of affordable (and undervalued) talent will feature smart and ambitious people who aren't yet experts in anything. With the right training and a supportive culture, they can become highly adaptive problem solvers—ideally, ones who perform well in teams. Those are the skills of generalists. This problem-solving flexibility will be essential because challenges and opportunities will change from one year to the next, or even faster than that.

Training not only enables companies to buy undervalued talent. It also dramatically widens the top of the funnel, which promises gains in diversity. If you're looking, for example, for a PhD in data science with experience in customer relationship management, you will not find much ethnic or gender diversity among the handful of top candidates. But if you're in the market for smart and ambitious people who are eager to learn, the talent pool widens. It's full of all kinds of candidates.

A showcase for this is a technology company, Akamai, a half-hour drive from our headquarters near Boston. Akamai, which came out of MIT, is a hotbed of advanced technology. The company delivers 15 to 30 percent of all online traffic, while providing cloud and security services. Like many tech companies, Akamai until recently faced serious diversity issues. Only 13 percent of the employees were female, while most racial and ethnic minorities were woefully underrepresented. The company hired Anthony Williams, its first diversity and inclusion leader. His task was to help Akamai bend the curve.*

Williams responded by laying out an ambitious educational initiative, and selling it to top management. The company went on to establish the Akamai Technical Academy in Cambridge. Promising candidates with scant digital skills go through a paid six-month training program onsite at Akamai. After that, candidates work at the company for several months on a contract basis, and the company hires some of them for full-time positions.† Naturally, these jobs aren't at technology's bleeding edge. But still, the training adds diversity to the workforce, which is a step forward.

---

* https://www.akamai.com/us/en/about/news/press/2019-press/akamai -technologies-appoints-anthony-williams-as-chief-human-resources-officer .jsp.

† https://workingnation.com/no-experience-required-building-a-new -digital-workforce/.

As companies focus on training and coaching, they become de facto educational institutions. In certain quarters, this has been true for decades. IBM, for example, is famous for developing talent. General Electric for a time was an incubator for executives. Corporate boards were much more likely to settle on a CEO or other top executive with such bona fides. They had an inkling of what they were getting.

The same holds true for managers who hire military veterans. Former Marines, a hiring manager knows, are likely to be resilient, respectful of hierarchy, and team players. That's the culture from which they come.

In the same way, companies of all sizes will be developing their cultural and educational brands. Some will be providing twenty-first-century vocational education, either to accompany a university curriculum or even to supplant it. Workers will advance in their lives and careers, some inside the company, others elsewhere. Those coming from great workplaces will share skills and culture, a common pedigree. These companies will function much like university alumni associations.

But what is a company at its essence? Does it make products? Provide services? Yes, of course. Those are its sources of revenue, which are vital. But does its line of business define it?

My answer is no. The essence of a company is the team of people it develops and motivates, and the culture that they share. This team can switch from one line of business to the next, but the foundational work, the key to success, is to build the dream teams that drive those companies. Everything else follows.

The temptation might be to recognize this truth—much the way we accept that a healthy diet and daily exercise are good for us—and then sit on it. After all, the status quo has its comforts. The HR department grinds on. The standard hiring process, while wracked with bias, delivers a few winners. Following my prescribed steps for optimizing data might be disruptive.

Take it from me, they *will* be disruptive. But in an ever-more competitive knowledge economy, the word is out there, both on fabulous and miserable places to work. People hear about organizations where people can grow and thrive, about about others where much is left to chance. The best talent will flow to the smartest and most welcoming workplaces. They'll fit into dream teams and deliver consistent winning performance.

A financial plan is indispensable. So is a strategy. Talent is the third leg of the stool, and no less necessary. I'd say more necessary.

I urge you to take action. Yes, it will take time and hard work to optimize talent in every aspect, from hiring to design. But you can kick-start the process by getting to know yourself and your team, through both assessments and old-fashioned conversation. Where are your high and low points of emotional intelligence? What's on the back of your T-shirt? Once you start to learn more about yourself, it'll seem only natural to extend that science to the rest of your organization. You'll be on your way to building a dream team.

ACKNOWLEDGMENTS

I t is only appropriate in a book about dream teams for me to fully acknowledge the fact that I have been so fortunate to have been surrounded by amazing people who have positively shaped my view of the world, of business, and of talent.

My deepest gratitude to my collaborator in this endeavor, Stephen Baker. You are a joy to work with and a master of the craft of writing.

A heartfelt thanks to my business partner for 17 years, Daniel Muzquiz. We have been through so much together—joys and frustrations, laughs and tears, successes and failures—and we have always remained friends. It's exactly what we set out to do. You have taught me a lot, *hermano*.

This book is dedicated to my friend and wife, Conley. She was the one who first introduced me properly to the use and power of psychometrics. This journey would not have happened without your support.

A special thank-you to Jackie Dube, my first and best strategic HR partner. Through 10 years of experimentation with real people and real teams, it has been an enjoyable journey figuring out talent optimization with you. We have come a long way since the early days. Remember, "Estimate how much oxygen is in the earth's atmosphere"? We can and did do better than that.

To my mighty colleagues at The Predictive Index, thought leaders all. You are doing wonderful things at PI, and daily you push me and each other for our mission of Better Work, Better World. Drew Fortin, for encouraging me to write this book in the first place. Matt Poepsel, for your insights into culture, leadership, and the armed forces. Drew and Matt in particular, for the gift of the talent optimization framework. Will Otto and Kristen Robertson, for your continual development of best practices around hiring and onboarding. Lindsey and Steve, for your contributions to design. Jenny for your support in promoting talent optimization and this book. Dana and Ali—brilliant scientists who helped shape my thinking. To a former PIoneer and my favorite Maverick PhD, Dr. Greg Barnett, who helped me make sense of this fragmented world. And of course Catherine McGurrin, whose logistical support has enabled this book to move to the end zone.

It is important to thank the young management team at LEDCO: Jamie Milligan, Brett Unzicker, Nic Milani, and Jay Shaw. We made so many management and leadership mistakes with you all, but we did create a stunning team.

There are many family members, teachers, coaches, and colleagues who were sources of inspiration. Thank you, Pat Dye, the high school English teacher who pushed me (and it was a long push). To my mom and dad, who gave me a love for learning and business, and every opportunity in the world. To Gary Bodie, for encouraging me to think beyond sailing. To Zack Leonard, for coaching me in so many ways. I do not think I would have gone to business school without you. To Chip Johns, for being a great first boss and business mentor. To Michael Allosso, who uses his considerable superpowers of perception for good and not evil, for giving the world TSP, and for pushing us all to be us on our best day. To my Vistage Chair, Bev Halperin, for helping me set higher bars. To my Vistage peers, for caring enough to give tough feedback. To Jim Allen, who was the genius behind Front of T-Shirt, Back of T-Shirt.

To members of the PI partner network who were critical in shaping my views of people and talent consulting: Heather Haas, Stan Kulfan, Dave Lahey, Jennifer Mackin, and, yes, even Steve Picarde.

And special thanks to Jim Levine, a great agent who was so helpful in helping hone this idea, and Casey Ebro, the talented editor who took a chance on this book and guided it through. I would also like to thank Kevin Maney, a great writer who helped shape the rough idea of this book.

APPENDIX

TALENT MANAGEMENT PERSONALITY/ BEHAVIORAL ASSESSMENTS

Personality and behavioral assessments are designed to provide scientifically based data about how people will behave and perform, as well as insights into the "why" behind those behaviors. Companies that need to hire the best talent, develop their employees, improve team functioning, and coach their leaders know that these tools provide a competitive advantage in their quest to build high-performance organizations. Here are our top five.

Talent Management Personality/Behavioral Assessments

Name	Why We Like It	Pros	Cons
Hogan Assessment Suite	Hogan Assessment Systems has made the "science of personality" its mission for decades. Hogan offers three well-designed assessments that, when used together, provide a comprehensive workplace personality assessment. One unique offering, Hogan Development Survey, taps into the dark side of personality and highlights how someone may derail their career. While Hogan's assessments are used in selection, the value of its solution is strongest in leadership development and executive selection.	• Executive coaches and advanced users value the in-depth level of analysis, with over 28 scales measuring day-to-day personality, potential derailers, and values. • Leaders appreciate the rich reporting content and the professional design of all materials. • The assessment of the dark side offers insights and opens dialogue about topics that are often difficult to discuss in the workplace.	• The length of the assessments (e.g., about 600 items) may be intimidating to candidates and other test-takers. • Managers and recruiters might struggle to gain value because of the complexity and information overload. • Measuring sensitive topics requires expertise and limits how broadly it can be used.

Talent Management Personality/Behavioral Assessments (continued)

Name	Why We Like It	Pros	Cons
The Predictive Index Behavioral Assessment (BA)	The Predictive Index Behavioral Assessment represents a combination of scientific rigor and simplicity, which makes it versatile. Used in business for more than 60 years, the BA can be completed quickly (six minutes) to support hiring, development, and team building. Because the results are easy to understand and memorable, the BA can be used beyond Human Resources. Managers and employees refer to it as part of their everyday interactions to better understand and work together.	• HR professionals will appreciate the BA's flexibility. Instead of relying on many different assessments, they can utilize one tool across most of their mission-critical talent management activities. • The BA has a number of different outputs and reporting designs that make it accessible to both novices and experts. • The BA doesn't ask inappropriate questions and takes only six minutes on average.	• The four-factor model the BA is based on is not as widely accepted by the scientific community. • The BA is a broad measure of behavioral tendencies, so it isn't comprehensive enough for more rigorous leadership coaching. • It measures the strongest personality drive within each individual, which makes it less ideal for comparing people side by side. • The results of the BA tend to be heavily focused on positive strengths, which may not be ideal for all use cases.
SHL Occupational Personality Questionnaire (OPQ32)	When it comes to the rigorous measurement of normal personality, the OPQ32 has been a market leader for decades. Initially developed in 1984 by SHL, the OPQ32 is one of the most widely used personality assessments in the world. Through the years it has been refined constantly to meet high standards of psychometric rigor and passed independent peer reviews in many countries. What makes the OPQ32 strong is its in-depth measurement of 32 different narrow traits, the availability of different versions for different use cases, and the sheer amount of data that has been collected through the years. This translates into valuable talent intelligence for clients.	• Clients value the versatility of the OPQ32 as it can be used in selection, development, team building, succession planning, and organizational change. • The extensive research, psychometric analysis, and wealth of data give confidence to more sophisticated users. • The ability to evaluate or develop talent along 32 different personality-based dimensions provides an in-depth view of a person. • SHL has over 14 different reports available, including its Universal Competency report, which makes it easy to understand talent potential in a business language.	• The OPQ32 can take 30 minutes to complete, something that can turn off employees and candidates. • Buyers can find the sheer number of different versions and reports confusing. • Understanding and interpreting 32 different personality characteristics can lead to information overload. • The OPQ32 results are complex, which limits its use as a tool that managers and employees can use more frequently.

Talent Management Personality/Behavioral Assessments (continued)

Name	Why We Like It	Pros	Cons
Caliper Profile	The Caliper Profile is an in-depth personality assessment that has been validated through 60 years of research. In addition to measuring 21 behavioral traits and motivations, it also includes a measure of cognitive ability. This makes the Caliper Profile a one-stop-shop tool for a variety of high-stakes talent decision and talent development purposes. The Caliper Profile is available in 24 languages and provides strong local norms for use in different countries. While the assessment is quite rigorous, Caliper aligns measurements with competencies, which makes it easier to use in hiring and for interpretation.	• Talent decision makers value the level of rigor that the Caliper Profile provides, especially in employee selection. • The Caliper Profile uses a format that reduces the likelihood of faking. • Managers and HR professionals appreciate the straightforward reporting that focuses results around recognizable business competencies. • Caliper provides additional tools, including behavioral interview guides, talent analytics, and individual development resources.	• Because it takes an average time of 60 minutes to complete, a number of candidates and employees may not finish it. • The design forces test-takers to make choices that can feel unnatural, further hurting the candidate experience. • The inclusion of a measure of cognitive ability raises legal risk because these may lead to adverse impacts more frequently than personality-based tools. • While the competency-based outputs are helpful for talent management, the Caliper Profile is still too complex to be used in an everyday manner and, in many cases, requires training or expert consultation.
The Birkman Method	The Birkman Method is another psychometrically rigorous personality-oriented assessment. While some assessments try to measure all aspects of personality, the Birkman Method has taken a slightly different approach, evaluating career interests, needs (motivations), usual behaviors, and stress behaviors. When taken together, the assessment focuses both on the people and on the environment and occupation that they are in. This allows for different insights, including work satisfaction and potentially career-limiting reactions to stress. While the Birkman Method can be used for hiring, team effectiveness, and career exploration, it shines in leadership development and executive coaching, where a deeper self-understanding is critical to successful growth.	• People seeking development and executive coaches value the insights that cover interests and stress behaviors. • The Birkman Method reports are easy to read and understand. • HR professionals appreciate the Birkman Method's focus on aligning people with their specific roles. • Birkman has done a strong job modernizing and increasing the psychometric rigor of its 60+-year-old assessment, and has passed a third-party audit. • The positive psychology foundation of the Birkman Method focuses on finding the best way to maximize one's work and life satisfaction.	• While not as long as some, the Birkman Method still takes 30 minutes on average to complete, which is not the ideal test-taking experience. • The Birkman Method isn't strong for higher-volume selection and is designed more as an interpretation tool than a decision-making one. • Companies will need to be trained or hire a consultant to get the most value. • It covers many aspects of personality, which makes it a more difficult tool to apply for more everyday uses.

OTHER ASSESSMENT METHODS

As technology, availability of data, and talent assessment sophistication have increased, so have different and valuable ways to assess and understand behavior in the workplace. When evaluating talent for hiring or development, a number of different methods and tools can provide valuable insights. The categories below are worth exploring.

Other Assessment Methods

Name	General Description	How It's Different	Potential Downsides
Gamification	Historically, most types of assessments have relied on standard survey style approaches, such as true/false, agree/disagree, for collecting talent data. Such assessments tend to be easier for test-takers to manipulate since the preferred answers are often obvious. But technology has opened new possibilities. Companies like Pymetrics and Arctic Shores have built game-like assessments for talent decision-making processes. These tools typically measure personality and cognitive ability but do so using short, interactive experiences that measure how an individual plays the game itself.	• Gamified assessments offer a positive candidate experience and reflect positively on the employer brand. • Gamification providers are able to collect myriad data points based on everything a test-taker does in a game. This allows for some unique insights and measurements into human potential. • Results are less likely to be impacted by conscious or unconscious biases that people have when taking assessments.	• Not everyone likes playing games during the application process. They can lead candidates to question what it has to do with the job. Games could be a turnoff for older people as well. • Gamified assessments tend to have a black box AI feel to them, meaning that their results are hard to explain. There is growing criticism and even new legislation as a backlash to this trend. • They raise questions about whether new is really better. While more standard survey-style assessments may be less fun, they are tried and true and tend to work quite well.

Other Assessment Methods (continued)

Name	General Description	How It's Different	Potential Downsides
Competency Frameworks	Competency frameworks aren't really assessments, but they do include assessment methodology. They function as blueprints for organizations to determine which characteristics, behaviors, and skills are needed for success in jobs, in leaders, or across an organization. What makes competency frameworks effective is their ability to communicate performance expectations in a simple and business-relevant way. Once a competency model has been defined, companies can develop or buy assessment tools that measure potential or performance against the competencies. They can also purchase or build their own training and learning tools to help employees improve in those key competency areas. Some companies such as Korn Ferry and SHL have developed entire talent solutions around competency frameworks that allow companies to define a job, identify what's needed for the job, measure potential in the job, and ultimately evaluate performance all in the same competency language.	• Competency frameworks aren't assessments, but they do make using assessments easier and more effective. • Instead of using assessment tools that measure and report results in their own particular language, competency frameworks create a common language to understand candidate potential or areas of development. • Whereas assessments are about predicting success in a role, competency frameworks are really about defining what success looks like in the first place. • When a company uses a competency framework effectively, it can allow for data from various assessment tools to be used together; for example, comparing personality results to 360 results.	• Competency frameworks can be complicated to implement. Companies have to make decisions based on whether they will be built around a job, job family, or leadership level, as well as whether they focus on technical matters or functional matters. • Companies can have a hard time finalizing their competency frameworks as many competencies seem important to success. Choosing the final list can take longer than expected. • Often, companies want their assessment results to be provided in competency language. This can lead to a loss of information as scientifically rigorous tools are translated to fit the competency model.

Other Assessment Methods (continued)

Name	General Description	How It's Different	Potential Downsides
Scrapers	With the advent of machine learning, natural language processing, and the sheer volume of available social media data, social scraping was born. Initially, social scraping started as an experiment between data science and marketing, as companies tried to understand their consumers and their sentiments toward their products and brands. As technology matured, so did the science. This led psychologists and entrepreneurs to develop personality profiles solely on the basis of peoples' social media activity. Companies like Crystal Knows and IBM (Watson Personality Insights) have developed tools that review Twitter, Facebook, and/or LinkedIn to generate personality profiles. It's controversial and can be misused. In 2016, Cambridge Analytica used Facebook data to develop personality profiles for targeted political ads. Companies also scrape LinkedIn to find passive candidates based on skills or experience, or use social scraping to vet job candidates for red flags, such as drug use or racism.	• By not requiring an individual to complete an assessment, social scraping represents a more efficient way to understand people. • While some high-stakes selection systems take 60 minutes, social scrapers attempt to provide similar value in seconds. • Natural-language processing and machine learning are rapidly evolving fields which means that social scraping tools are improving at a much higher velocity than standard assessments. • There is a wow factor to social scraping, especially if the results ring true. This generates excitement and enthusiasm that rarely accompanies traditional psychometric tools. • Social scraping makes it possible to identify how well passive candidates will fit a job before even talking to them. This is already being done with experience data, but could soon be used for personality-based fit as well.	• Serious moral and ethical issues will continue to challenge the broad acceptance of social scraping. • Social scrapers measuring personality characteristics tend to suffer from accuracy issues. Tried-and-true assessments yield more valid results. • Social scraping technology only works if there is data to be found. Not all people have the same social media footprint. • As this technology continues to mature, people are becoming savvier about their publicly available information. This means that careful social media profile management could lead users to generate conclusions that are incorrect.

Other Assessment Methods (continued)

Name	General Description	How It's Different	Potential Downsides
Video/Audio Interviews	Interviews remain the primary method by which talent is evaluated for recruitment and hiring. Video and audio interviews are on the rise as critical assessment tools in modern employee selection processes. In their simplest form, these assessments make it easy for candidates to interview remotely or asynchronously, recording answers to a slate of interview questions. Recruiters and hiring managers can watch, listen, or read the transcript of responses at their convenience. The uniform questions add scientific rigor. Hiring managers can more easily rate and compare the responses. Also, advances in machine learning and natural language processing have led to solutions that evaluate what people say, how they say it, and even their face and body language. These AI solutions are often criticized, but the field is young. More will be done in the coming years to remove humans from the interviewing process.	• These formats utilize technology to create better remote interviews. • More advanced technology allows companies to conduct structured interviews at scale by using asynchronous interviews that record responses to predetermined questions. Beyond convenience, this also allows a company to conduct more interviews with more candidates because they impose fewer time constraints. • Standard interviews are fraught with opportunities for unconscious bias and other problems that introduce error. But video and audio interviews allow users to replay responses, provide ratings, and even take notes in ways that follow best practices in conducting high-caliber interviews. • In addition, as people become more used to video-based communication, it is an experience that will become increasingly more acceptable, and preferable to long commutes for in-person interviews.	• Without real-time communication, candidates cannot clarify their responses, and interviewers cannot use the time to help sell the role. • AI-based video interviewing has come under heavy legal and political scrutiny. Some research suggests that AI-based interviews are biased against people of color. • The analysis within the AI is something of a black box. This means that recommendations against someone cannot be easily explained. There will be a battle in this area for some time to come, which may slow its acceptance.

Other Assessment Methods (*continued*)

Name	General Description	How It's Different	Potential Downsides
Simulations	Simulations provide a way to test job candidates by having them perform the role. While "simulation" conjures up images of VR and avatars, these trials have a rich history in employee selection. For decades, industrial and manufacturing companies tested candidates' speed, strength, and dexterity on task simulations. Managers often faced tryouts featuring "in-basket" simulations. While predictive, simulations were resource-intensive, time-consuming, and expensive. Technology now makes it possible to build high-fidelity work situations that not only capture the essence of the job but also remove the need for in-person assessment or human raters. Today, simulations can provide technically sound and engaging experiences that accurately predict job performance across a number of roles. And as VR and AR become more prominent, it is expected that simulations will continue to become more realistic, interactive, and capable of measuring potential in ways that traditional assessments cannot.	• Unlike other assessments that make predictions based on test scores, simulations predict job performance based on actual performance on highly job-relevant tasks. This makes them very accurate. • Simulations, especially with today's technology, can be fun and engaging for candidates. Not only does this improve the recruitment experience, it can help a company reinforce its own hiring brand, especially for newer generations of job seekers. • Many simulations also serve as a realistic job preview, meaning candidates get a taste of what the job they are applying for is actually like. This can help weed out candidates who realize that the work they might be doing isn't for them.	• Simulations tend to be better for some roles than others. For example, simulations excel in predicting performance in jobs heavy on routine and process, like call centers. But for leadership and managerial roles, there is more complexity to success, which simulations cannot always model or measure. • Simulations can be expensive and time-consuming to create, especially when a company wants one that feels cutting edge. • Simulations tend to be best for large companies hiring at high volumes for a specific role. Small and medium-sized businesses that hire for less specialized roles and lower volumes are unlikely to find simulations to be a good fit for their hiring practices.

COGNITIVE ASSESSMENTS

Cognitive ability assessments are based on nearly a century of research and represent the single best assessment-based predictor of job performance. Cognitive ability largely relates to how fast a person learns, catches on, and figures things out on the job. Most workplace cognitive ability assessments involve a combination of verbal, math/numeric, pattern, and logic-based problems to answer within a limited time. Each correct answer raises the score. While cognitive assessments can predict job performance, they have two downsides. First, the timed nature can be intense and stressful to test-takers, which can sour their experience. Second, most research shows that some demographic groups tend to score lower on these tests, which can lead to unfair hiring practices. It is important to understand the legal implications of the assessments. Below are some of the best.

Cognitive Assessments

Name	General Description	How It's Different	Potential Downsides
Wonderlic Contemporary Cognitive Ability Test (WCCAT)	The Wonderlic Contemporary Cognitive Ability Test, formerly known as the Wonderlic Personnel Test, is the grandfather of all timed workplace cognitive assessments. The assessment has been around since 1936 and has seen a number of changes and improvements. The current version is 50 items long with a 12-minute time limit. Items cover vocabulary and reading comprehension, basic arithmetic and word problems, formal logic, and general knowledge questions.	• Because of the sheer volume of data Wonderlic has collected over the years, it has data insights and norms for nearly every job in the US economy. • Wonderlic offers an online 8-minute version of its cognitive assessment, which is designed to be used before candidates come in. • Since the WCCAT has been in use for decades, Wonderlic is able to provide strong expertise with regard to implementation and legal issues for nearly all scenarios.	• Wonderlic (the company) has recently moved away from selling the cognitive assessment on its own. The new business model features a single score based on cognitive, personality, and motivation assessments. This limits the availability of information specific to the newest version of the cognitive portion. • Wonderlic supports a limited number of languages, which limits its widespread global use.

Cognitive Assessments (continued)

Name	General Description	How It's Different	Potential Downsides
PI Cognitive Assessment	The PI Cognitive Assessment is a well-designed, scientifically rigorous measure of cognitive ability that has been peer-reviewed and certified in third-party audits. Like Wonderlic, the PI Cognitive Assessment uses a similar 12-minute, 50-item approach to measuring cognitive ability. It focuses on numerical, verbal, and abstract reasoning to produce candidate scores.	• The PI Cognitive Assessment is designed specifically for hiring decisions, so it comes with a complete methodology that includes a cognitive job analysis to help companies find the right scoring ranges for each job. • The assessment uses a dynamic test engine which generates a unique version of the assessment for each test-taker. This increases the security of the assessment and also makes it easier to readminister a different version in case something goes wrong. • It is global. It has been translated into over 70 languages and is in use in 120 countries worldwide.	• The PI Cognitive Assessment is designed to be administered with the PI Behavioral Assessment, so it may not be the best option when a company is looking only for a cognitive test. • Some organizations like to use norms and averages by industry or job type. The PI Cognitive Assessment is limited in this area.

Cognitive Assessments (*continued*)

Name	General Description	How It's Different	Potential Downsides
Saville Technical Aptitude Tests	Saville offers an entire library of specific ability assessments designed for particular roles or job-levels. While the Saville Technical Aptitude tests range from 6 minutes to 24 minutes, its most popular test (the Swift Analysis Aptitude) takes 18 minutes to complete.	• Even though the item types are similar, Saville's increased length can provide more than just an overall cognitive ability score. Many of its tests measure verbal, numeric, and pattern recognition abilities, which, together, can provide a more nuanced view of a person's cognitive ability. This is important when a job role leans toward a specific aptitude (e.g., accountant and numerical ability). • Saville offers tests that have specific use cases. For example, the Professional Verbal Analysis is a 20-minute in-depth assessment that measures language ability, whereas the Error Checking Aptitude is a short 6-minute test designed for entry or apprentice-level roles.	• Research has long shown that overall cognitive ability scores tend to be highly correlated with all facets of cognitive ability, so Saville's depth may be unnecessary. • Cognitive ability assessments are notoriously intense for people to complete. The 12-minute versions are already a challenging candidate experience. The 18- and 24-minute versions could be too grueling for some candidates.

Cognitive Assessments (continued)

Name	General Description	How It's Different	Potential Downsides
Raven's Progressive Matrices (RPM)	First published in 1938, Raven's Progressive Matrices is one of the original cognitive assessments. While modernized significantly in recent years, it remains unique in that it is designed to measure only abstract reasoning (fluid intelligence) versus the standard numerical and verbal reasoning. The abstract items are all multiple choice and involve asking a person to identify the missing element (i.e., a picture) that completes a pattern of shapes. It's important to note that RPM has different versions and uses, including the Raven's Standard Progressive Matrices, Colored Progressive Matrices (for children, the elderly, or mentally impaired individuals), and Advanced Progressive Matrices (for adults and adolescents of above-average intelligence). As such, while it is popular in preemployment selection, it also has numerous clinical applications, such as predicting educational attainment for children and students.	• Because RPM doesn't use language or numbers, it is independent of reading and writing skills. For this reason, it tends to reduce cultural bias and is easier to implement in any language or culture. • RPM is not timed, so it doesn't create the same stressful testing experience as do timed cognitive assessments. • RPM has been part of a significant amount of peer-reviewed academic research.	• RPM may be untimed, but it still takes a significant period to complete. The Standard version takes 20–45 minutes, while the Advanced version averages 40–60 minutes. That's a lot of time to devote to one assessment and enough to cause candidate drop-off in many selection systems. • RPM is generally offered through Pearson as a stand-alone assessment that requires test booklets and answer sheets. While it can be taken online, it won't have robust reporting or be easily integrated into an online candidate selection process.

Cognitive Assessments (continued)

Name	General Description	How It's Different	Potential Downsides
Watson-Glaser Critical Thinking Appraisal	While many timed cognitive assessments are built to measure broad cognitive ability, the Watson-Glaser is uniquely designed to go deep in a specific area: critical thinking. The newest version of the Watson-Glaser Critical Thinking Appraisal is a 30-minute assessment designed specifically for verbal ability questions. Specifically, the Watson-Glaser is used to evaluate a candidate's ability to think critically, draw conclusions, assess strong and weak arguments, recognize assumptions, and evaluate arguments. It is built using multiple-choice questions that provide a scenario or a short statement. Candidates then must make ratings such as whether a statement is true or false (including an insufficient data option) or whether a statement makes a strong or weak argument. While the Watson-Glaser can be used for hiring employees in all roles, the focus on critical thinking makes it particularly useful for roles that have wider discretion in decision-making and judgment.	• The Watson-Glaser has a timed version for employee selection purposes and an untimed version for development purposes. • The newest version of the Watson-Glaser has a large item bank by which it randomly selects questions making it unlikely that two individuals receive the same test. This is a strong feature for test security. • The results are reported against a relevant norm in order to determine whether someone is high, average, or low on critical thinking. There are many available norms for comparison making the Watson-Glaser useful for making decisions across a number of job roles.	• Whether timed or untimed, the Watson-Glaser is an intensive and lengthy test experience. It is likely that a number of candidates will not enjoy this type of assessment. • While the Watson-Glaser measures critical thinking, research shows that scores on it correlate highly with other, shorter cognitive assessments. It may be beneficial for some roles, but better options exist for higher volume selection. • Because it is a fully verbal assessment, it is likely to have more cultural bias than other assessments and may not be as valid for people who are slow readers. In addition, it is currently only available in nine languages.

CONSUMER-GRADE PSYCHOMETRICS

Some of the most popular types of assessments aren't necessarily the most scientifically rigorous. These "consumer-grade" tools tend to be simple, memorable, and attractive to talent management professionals. They are not really designed to be used in high-stakes hiring situations but do serve a broader purpose in helping people to become self-aware, communicate, and work better together. Below are some of the most common assessments on the market.

Consumer-Grade Psychometrics

Name	General Description	What We Like	Potential Downsides
Myers-Briggs Type Indicator (MBTI)	The MBTI is the most popular assessment in the world. It's not just famous because many millions of people have completed it. It's because millions of people remember their MBTI profiles scores for most of their life. That kind of sticking power means that it becomes the personality model that most know and compare other assessment results against.	• Many, especially those with limited assessment experience, enjoy the simple four-letter profile that the MBTI provides. It is memorable and provides quick insight and self-awareness. • The MBTI is versatile. It can be used as a part of executive coaching all the way down to improving team dynamics, relationships, and employee performance. • HR and other talent professionals appreciate the safe nature of the MBTI. It focuses on strengths and can be administered without a lot of oversight and control.	• The MBTI is quite controversial in science circles with many studies showing that it lacks reliability. This means scores tend to change when people retake it. • The MBTI uses a typology to provide scores, which means it isn't very precise. You can either be an Extravert or an Introvert vs. other tools that tell you where on the continuum you fall. • Because the MBTI is so popular, it often becomes the first assessment experience people have. This is potentially problematic when companies introduce more rigorous tools and people don't trust the results because they differ from what they've already internalized as their true personality.

Consumer-Grade Psychometrics *(continued)*

Name	General Description	What We Like	Potential Downsides
DISC	There are many different versions of the DISC and many different vendors selling it. So while the DISC may appear to be among the most popular assessments in the world, it is actually the DISC model that has become so prevalent. The DISC is popular because it provides a simple way of understanding who people are and how they will show up at work. The information is consumable by everyday employees and managers, and the results tend to be remembered long after the assessment results are provided.	• The DISC provides a high-level understanding of behavioral tendencies around 4 primary drives and 12 personality types, with many versions providing those results using an attractive circle-based graphic that assessment beginners instantly understand. • The DISC is the type of tool that can be used as part of everyday work in terms of understanding work styles, relationships, team composition, and more. • Talent management professionals value the flexibility of the tool and the aha moments it delivers without the need to provide extensive training or structured learning. • Many versions of the DISC exist, but Everything DISC by Wiley Publishing provides extensive reporting tools and online development resources that give users at all levels and roles an impactful growth experience.	• The DISC is based on a 60-year old model of personality that doesn't align with modern psychological research. It works, but there are more accurate ways to assess personality. • Because of the multitude of DISC vendors, there is a lot of variation in terms of quality, accuracy, and value. It is quite easy for someone to take two different DISCs and end up with different scores. • As with the MBTI, the DISC is a great beginner's tool, but it can often lead to first impressions that become the standard by which all other assessments are compared. People can be hesitant to trust other results. • People fall in love with tools like the DISC, but that can lead to misuse. For example, the DISC wasn't designed to be used for employee selection, but many people value the results enough to use it for this purpose.

Consumer-Grade Psychometrics *(continued)*

Name	General Description	What We Like	Potential Downsides
Grit	In recent years, Grit has become one of the most highly sought-after characteristics in candidates and employees across all roles, levels, and industries. Broadly defined as passion and perseverance for long-term and meaningful goals, the popularity of grit has exploded in large part due to the books and research of Angela Duckworth. For her research, Duckworth designed a Grit assessment that has steadily become part of mainstream talent assessment. Still, in today's talent assessment industry, organizations are frequently trying to hire for grit, even without using a grit-specific assessment.	• What makes Grit great for HR and talent professionals is that it has instant meaning to managers and leaders. Whether for selection or development, there are few psychological constructs that are so easily understood and accepted as key performance differentiators. • Because many people believe in the value of Grit, it has helped increase the adoption of assessments in the hiring process, even for those who tend to be skeptical of talent assessments. • Grit, at least Duckworth's version, has research showing that it isn't just a fad, that it predicts meaningful work outcomes like job performance and work satisfaction.	• The most commonly used Grit assessment (i.e., Duckworth's) isn't really designed for employee selection. It is short and transparent, which means it is easy to fake. • Academics have serious reservations about Grit. First, some studies show that Grit is just conscientiousness repackaged, and therefore current tests designed to measure conscientiousness in applicants are superior. Second, academic studies have found contradictory evidence about how well Grit predicts job performance. This suggests that its popularity isn't backed up by science.

Consumer-Grade Psychometrics (continued)

Name	General Description	What We Like	Potential Downsides
Emotional Intelligence (EQ)	Emotional Intelligence assessments, of which there are many, aren't all "consumer-grade" psychometrics. Some are well-designed psychometric tools. However, the "emotional intelligence" concept has become so popular that the measurement and understanding of it have become largely diluted by pop psychology. It was initially coined in 1990 by Peter Salovey and John D. Mayer as a "a form of social intelligence that involves the ability to monitor one's own and others' feelings and emotions, to discriminate among them, and to use this information to guide one's thinking and action." Today, Emotional Intelligence is considered by many to be the secret to interpersonal and leadership success. Consequently, an entire industry emerged, including hundreds of books, tests, and training programs devoted to understanding and developing it. From an assessment perspective, three types of emotional intelligence evaluation tools exist. Personality-based emotional intelligence tests (e.g., the EQ-I) which measures EQ traits, ability-based versions (e.g., the MSCEIT) that test EQ like it is a skill, and 360-degree feedback tools that gather feedback on a person's emotional intelligence at work.	• Emotional Intelligence has the attention of business leaders and HR professionals. This makes it an easier type of tool to bring into talent management processes than other types of assessments. • According to a number of academic studies, Emotional Intelligence is an adequate predictor of job performance. While it isn't designed to be used in high-volume selection, understanding leaders' potential EQ can add valuable data to high-stakes decisions. • There are a great number of EQ assessment tools. They provide talent management professionals with many options on how to bring EQ measurement into their organizations. • EQ can be developed and coached. Unlike some tests, like cognitive, an EQ assessment can be a starting point for important personal growth.	• Because there are so many models and tests for EQ, it isn't clear what it really is. Is it a personality trait or an ability? Which of the many EQ tests measures it the right way? These questions aren't game stoppers, but they are warnings that EQ isn't just one thing. Care must be taken to understand the specific EQ model and test that is being used. • A lot of research suggests that EQ may just be a rebrand of old concepts. Studies find that familiar personality characteristics and cognitive ability largely account for any variation in predicting job performance. Since this is the case, experts advocate for using what is proven rather than getting caught up in the highly commercialized EQ world.

Consumer-Grade Psychometrics *(continued)*

Name	General Description	What We Like	Potential Downsides
Clifton-Strengths (aka Strengths-Finder)	Formerly called Clifton StrengthsFinder, the CliftonStrengths Assessment is a widely used assessment that is a foundational tool in the strengths-based psychology movement. Designed as a self-awareness and development tool, CliftonStrengths provides users with insight into which of 34 themes best define their greatest talents. They then can put them to work to achieve success, excellence, and life satisfaction. CliftonStrengths reports results by providing people with a rank order of the 34 themes, but ultimately puts most of the emphasis on the top 5 as the key to understanding what makes them unique. Because CliftonStrengths is owned by Gallup, the tools have been connected to a number of interesting findings related to manager behavior and employee engagement.	• The focus on strengths makes CliftonStrengths a safe assessment to introduce into nearly any type of organization. People tend to share their results openly. This encourages dialogue which improves relationships and understanding. • The assessment results are easy to consume and understand. The themes frame complex personality tendencies into memorable labels (e.g., Futuristic) that instantly communicate valuable information. The reporting aligns users with four simple categories, so that a clear interpretive story can be understood.	• CliftonStrengths doesn't provide scores on the themes it measures, only a rank. This type of black box raises questions about accuracy. For example, it is impossible to know if someone was truly high on themes compared to other people or if they are all just about average. • Further, because the top five themes are given considerable weight in reporting, there is no way to compare how much higher they really are compared to other themes. Psychometrics teach us that all assessments have measurement error, and there is a strong chance that the ranking could change significantly with a few small changes in responses.

FEEDBACK SYSTEMS

Talent assessments are powerful tools for understanding human behavior in the workplace. But they are limited in that they provide perspective only on individuals' tendencies, and not how they are performing, leading, or engaging with the organization's culture. It is important for companies to round out their talent data strategy by using feedback systems to monitor, measure, and give feedback related to the work experience. Companies should focus on three major areas to build a better talent management strategy.

Feedback Systems (continued)

Name	What They Are	How the Vendors Differ	Things You Should Know
360s	360-degree feedback, also known as multi-rater feedback, has been a mainstay in businesses for decades. The premise is simple. Employee feedback, typically in the form of ratings, is gathered from a variety of sources, including the employee (i.e., a self-rating) and the employee's subordinates, colleagues, and supervisor. Traditionally, the results were used for development, but in more recent years companies have been using them as a proxy for performance. The model-oriented 360s are excellent for leadership because they provide great benchmark data and strong resources to help leaders continue to grow and improve. They are less than ideal for lower-level roles as they often assess for leadership-level behaviors as opposed to those of managers or front-line employees.	• Some vendors provide well-thought-out models for collecting ratings such as Leadership Circles, the Extraordinary Leader 360, and the Leadership Versatility Index. These tools often come with extensive reporting, books, other developmental content, and coaching support. • An alternative approach, from vendors such as Echospan and Qualtrics, allows for highly customizable 360s. They typically come with a library of available items to use and advanced administration features that make data collection easier. • The vendors are effective when companies have their own competency model and simply need tools to administer their own content. They can also help savvy companies build 360s with very little effort. While the technology vendors may make collecting the data easier, they don't offer much guidance on what to do with it. Companies that use these types of tools need to invest time and resources into how to understand results and deliver feedback.	• 360s provide important insights because they facilitate the comparison of ratings from different rating sources. Employees are able to identify blind spots (i.e., self-ratings are higher than others), hidden strengths (i.e., self-ratings are lower than others), and group-specific differences (e.g., manager ratings are lower than everyone else). • The 360s provide open-ended comments, which can be rich in detail. The insights from comments can be more important than the ratings themselves. • Some rating biases dilute the value. Often, raters give overly positive scores, which leads to generally glowing results and failure to uncover strong areas for growth. • 360 fatigue is another concern. When managers have too many of these to complete, they either won't get them all done or, worse, put little thought and effort into the ratings they are giving.

Feedback Systems (continued)

Name	What They Are	How the Vendors Differ	Things You Should Know
Culture and Engagement	Culture and Engagement are broad topics that refer to the employee experience, the employee commitment to the organization, and the values that are reinforced and rewarded in the work environment. In short, it addresses the question: "What is it like to work here?" To scientifically answer this question, organizations traditionally use survey methodologies that involve asking employees their opinions and sentiment across a wide range of work-related items. The results are used to understand employee engagement levels, the elements that are driving or hurting engagement, cultural strengths and challenges, and other issues that are helping or hindering productivity. Historically, the most common approach to gathering this data has been an annual employee census, an in-depth survey the entire organization is asked to complete within a week or two. Today, advances in technology and science have made it easier to collect employee sentiment more frequently. This has led to vendors offering tools that allow for shorter pulse surveys, on-demand polls, and even real-time listening sessions, during which employees can provide feedback within the flow of their daily work.	• Companies like Energage, the Great Place to Work, and Quantum Workplace conduct annual surveys that allow companies to see how they compare to others benchmarked for excellence. While these companies can provide more in-depth services, their strength is the ability to use data to help companies understand how strong their culture is, or what they need to do to achieve greatness. In more recent years, Glassdoor has become a big player in this space as it collects ratings from employees and ex-employees to determine similar rankings. • Companies like Glint, Culture Amp, TINYpulse, and Emplify have invested heavily in cutting-edge technology that makes it easy to conduct surveys with a high degree of frequency. They also have advanced data science tools that can identify trends, analyze comments, predict future outcomes, and deliver insights to managers in real time. • Traditional, annual survey providers like Qualtrics, Towers Watson, and Gallup are experts in building and executing on the more complex engagement and culture initiatives. These vendors tend to have the infrastructure, logistical support (e.g., receiving mailed-in paper surveys), and consulting expertise to help big companies navigate the complexities effectively.	• Finding the right vendor is really about knowing where your company is in terms of maturity. If the annual survey is already a huge hassle to execute or has little leadership buy-in, then it may be best to keep it simple. The Top/Best/Great Workplace providers are a good start because they tend to be free and the results compare your organization with others, which might get leadership's competitive juices flowing. • Many people like the sound of real-time employee listening. In fact, it's what large consumer brands are doing with Twitter and Facebook. But it is important to balance listening with action. If employees perceive that their input is landing on deaf ears and they aren't seeing continual improvements, then it makes no sense to continually ask their opinion. • Survey data, in and of itself, will not build a better organization. Many of the vendors listed here offer best practices for next steps. But companies still struggle to make meaningful improvements a reality. It's important to invest time and resources into drawing lessons from the data *and* taking action.

Feedback Systems *(continued)*

Name	What They Are	How the Vendors Differ	Things You Should Know
Performance	Performance management is one of the most complicated and controversial topics in talent management. So it shouldn't be a surprise that performance feedback systems mirror the complexity. At one time, the annual performance appraisal reigned as the predominant methodology for managing and measuring employee performance. But research emerged showing that annual performance appraisals were ineffective at best, and often destructive. These findings set off a new paradigm of performance management that focused less on measuring performance and more on frequent feedback and coaching. Today, performance management practices vary greatly from organization to organization and so do the performance feedback systems designed to capture and make use of the data. That means finding the right vendor depends largely on the type of performance management approach that will work best in your organization. In addition, the performance management domain has expanded to include goal management and recognition systems as well.	• In 2018, 10 software vendors accounted for over 50 percent of the performance and goal management systems. These include companies like SAP, Cornerstone On-Demand, Saba, and Oracle, which provide performance tools as part of larger human capital management systems. These vendors offer many innovations but are generally complex to implement, since they tend to be designed for large enterprises. • Dozens of smaller vendors have emerged that provide lighter, more agile solutions. These include 15Five, Reflektive, and 7geese. They tend to offer solutions that use Objective and Key Results (OKR) frameworks to cascade goals throughout the organization. • Because of the sheer number of providers, it is impossible to differentiate the vendors much further. It's important to know that many performance vendors tend to stretch their offerings into adjacent spaces, such as employee engagement or human capital. For these reasons, vendor differentiation is partly about being strategic about additional talent needs that will benefit your company.	• Technology has made it easier than ever to deploy performance management solutions, but that doesn't mean it will be successful in your company. Performance management requires thoughtful implementation, alignment with your culture and business imperatives, and discipline from managers, leaders, and employees. • In the ongoing performance management debates, some argue against collecting any data at all. But without performance data, promotions, compensation decisions, and terminations are left to biased human decision-making. Not only does that lead to errors, but it could lead to legal problems if people are not treated equitably. • If your company is new to performance management, consider a crawl, walk, run approach. Start simple by implementing a process that increases conversation and communication between managers and employees. Next, formalize the process by introducing simplified goals that can be changed and updated on a frequent basis. The real key is getting people into the right habits first so that more process is seen as a value-add, rather than HR-driven control.

INDEX

ABOUT THE AUTHORS

Mike Zani is the CEO of The Predictive Index, a talent optimization company that uses behavioral, cognitive, and job assessments to make hiring, motivating, and managing people more efficient and effective. Its clients include AstraZeneca, Blue Cross Blue Shield, TD Bank, DocuSign, LVMH, and Omni Hotels, among many others. Zani is also a cofounder and partner at Phoenix Strategy Investments, a private investment fund. An avid sailor, he was a coach of the 1996 US Olympic Team. He holds a BS from Brown University and an MBA from Harvard Business School.

For more information, visit predictiveindex.com.

Stephen Baker was a senior technology writer at *Bloomberg Businessweek*. He is the author of *The Numerati* and *Final Jeopardy: Man vs. Machine and the Quest to Know Everything* and coauthor of the *New York Times* bestseller *Where Does It Hurt?: An Entrepreneur's Guide to Fixing Health Care* and *Hop, Skip, Go: How the Mobility Revolution Is Transforming Our Lives.*